The Condition of Seoul Architecture

Pier Alessio Rizzardi

TCA Think Tank

The Condition of Seoul Architecture

Author
Pier Alessio Rizzardi

Contributing Authors
Choi Won-Joon
John Hong
Caroline Maniaque Benton
Rafael Luna

Photographers
Iwan Baan
Kim Yong-kwan
Sun Nam-goong
Hwang Woo-seop

English Editor
Zhang Hankun

Korean Editor
Han So-young
Kim Betti

On the cover
Dongdaemun Plaza
Photo by Iwan Baan

ISBN-13: 978-1-9164537-3-9

tcathinktank.com

We are greatly thankful to:

Collaborators, scholars, and authors who shared their profound theoretical and practiced knowledge.
Rafael Luna, Choi Won-Joon, John Hong, Park Jin-hee, Jong Lee, Kim Sung-hong, Maniaque Caroline.

Architects and researchers, editors, curators, and journalists who shared their inspiring support and advise and widely contribute to the visibility of the research.
Kim Sung-hong, Sung Goosup, Cesare Maria Casati, Romolo Roberto Calabrese, Yim Dong-woo, Kim You-been.

Photographers who kindly contributed with their photographic endeavors.
Iwan Baan, Sun Nam-goong, Kim Yong-kwan, Hwang Woo-seop, Kim Jong-oh, Shin Kyung-sub, Song Jae-young, Ku Boun-sook, Kim Hee-su, Jennifer Bailey, Franzisco Anzola, Andrew Currie, Aleksander Zykov, Park Nam-ho, Hoon Yeum-seung, Hans Jan Dürr, Jean-Pierre Dalbéra, William A., Fernando Herrera, ang Jin-wook, Kim Jae-kyeong, Park Young-chae, Jeffry Sandy, Jua Chae, Eco Dalla Luna.

Institutions who believed, supported, showcased, and patronaged the research.
Seoul Biennale of Architecture and Urbanism, Future Cities Laboratory | ETH Zurich, STUDIO Architecture and Urbanism Magazine, l'ARCA International, ArchDaily, Designboom.

Protagonists of this story, who patiently agreed to discuss with us their essential thoughts.
Moon Hoon, Gyoo Jang-yoon, Kim Dong-jin & Kim Yoo-jung, Cho Min-suk, Kim Young-joon, Hwang Doo-jin, Kim In-cheurl, Cho Byoung-soo, Kim Min-ji, Kim Hyo-man, Kim Jun-sung, Choi Moon-gyu, Choi Wook, Kim Jong-kyu, Ken Sungjin-min, Kim Chan-joong, Kim Seung-hoy, Lee Jeong-hoon.

The material contained in the book was part of the exhibition at
Cities Exhibition for the Seoul Biennale of Architecture and Urbanism 2019,
from 7th September to 10th November 2019.

In collaboration with:

서울 도시건축 비엔날레
SEOUL BIENNALE OF ARCHITECTURE AND URBANISM

Supported by:

l'ARCA International Magazine

STUDIO Architecture
and Urbanism Magazine

Foreword

by Choi Won-joon

As architectural historian Jeon Bong-hee noted, Korea is currently witnessing, for the first time in its modern history, the coexistence of multiple generations of architects.[1] Architecture as a modern profession was established relatively late in Korea, as it was only in the 1950s that curricula for architecture became widespread in universities, producing what we call the first generation of Korean modern architects. However, their design careers were often cut short, for some key figures due to premature death but mostly because of a professional culture that tends to retire seniors or relegate them from design practice to managerial and executive duties in the name of promotion.

Hence we never had the opportunity to enjoy the richness and dynamism of a discipline that generational accumulation provides. That is, until recently: now we have architects in their 80s, from the very first generation, who are still active; on the other end, young practitioners, as we shall later see, who are opening their firms as soon as they reach their 30s, redefining the meaning and capacity of the so-called 'young architect'; and a wide range of age groups in between. To understand the contemporary architectural world of Korea, and to shed light on its participants, what ideals they pursue, and how they came about, we should look back as far as thirty years.

1

The late 1980s and the early 1990s were certainly a period of transition for the Korean society at large and its world of architecture. In politics, consistent protests for democracy of the previous decade finally bore fruit with the establishment of a civilian government—the first since the 1961 *coup d'état* and the subsequent military dictatorships—and in socio-cultural terms, the hosting of the Summer Olympic Games in 1988 and the liberalization of overseas travel in the following year opened up the eyes of the nation to the contemporary world scene. Years of record-setting economic growth created a strong middle class, the cultural awakening of which led to an expanding capitalist market of mass culture. The building industry, the driving force of national economy since the post-Korean War recovery years (claiming 25.4 percent of the GDP at its peak) and dominated by government-initiated grand projects throughout the 1980s in preparation of the Olympiad, was now flourishing with a growing private market, creating a situation where a rising number of architects were now competing in the design market in demand of novel styles. Architecture, once a matter of economy and engineering in a nation in dire need of economic development, was beginning to be accepted as a part of the cultural milieu in the public perception.

However, the response of the young generation of architects to this new condition was quite critical. Unconvinced of the validity of Postmodernism, a belated stylistic import through expanded channels of international exchange, to a nation that had yet to go through a proper process of cultural modernization, [2] they refused to follow ephemeral commercial trends and approached architecture as an act of cultural and social responsibility. Basing their beliefs in the modern ideal to change society and its way of life through architecture, many of them participated in group efforts for theoretical coalition or direct social engagement, with aims to reform the conservative nature of the architectural world and its bureaucratic systems.

Most active among these gatherings was 4.3 Group, consisting of fourteen architects then in their thirties and forties—among them Kim In-cheurl, the eldest practitioner interviewed in this publication. Many were protégés of Kim Swoo-ge-

un and Kim Chung-up, the pioneering figures of Korean modernism who suddenly passed away in 1986 and 1988 respectively, while others had just broken away from where they started their professional careers—large corporate-type design firms that claimed and still claims a major part of Korea's building industry. [3] In either case, they were ready and eager to stand on their own. Their individual quests to establish idiosyncratic voices and formal principles in an increasingly competitive market led them to support their designs with parallel productions in literary discourse, in the form of thematic project titles, essays, and manifestoes, presented in numerous journals, book publications, and "Echoes of an Era," an influential exhibition in 1992. [4] These theoretical projections, be it a recourse to modernist ideas, French Post-Structuralist theories, traditional Confucian ideals of asceticism, or their strange mixtures, featured an expansive breadth of references, from Western art to Eastern philosophy to media studies, successfully establishing architecture as an intellectual and cultural discipline. Yet their arguments rather converged into similar themes: issues of the void and the indeterminate in architecture, the origin of which can be found in Korea's traditional idea of space, especially in *Madang*, a surrounded courtyard of old residences characterized by the non-specificity of its function. This sharing of ideas also led to similar formal attributes as well, such as their preference for exposed concrete that fitted their austere ideals. Aware of and encouraged by the Regionalist movements of South America and Japan of the late-modern years, they continued to explore what is inherently Korean in architecture, thus extending into the 1990s the search for national identity and cultural heritage—a highly sensitive topic for the nation that underwent Japanese colonial rule in the early part of the twentieth century, during which its tradition and culture were forcefully suppressed and discontinued. Since the 1945 liberation until then, answers to these quests were rather limited, usually in the form of reproduction or pastiche of historical styles. Such formalist approach was now replaced with explorations on the more fundamental dimensions of spatial and programmatic organization, but the legacy of the grand narrative in pursuit of Koreanness persisted.

2

However, nearing the *fin-de-siècle*, a different response characterized a younger breed of emerging architects, to which many of this publication's interviewees belong. Setting up their own practices as early as the mid-1990s but mainly in the late 1990s and the early years of the twenty-first century, they were critical of the heavily philosophical, even sophisticated nature of architectural discourse as practiced by their seniors, and the homogenous theories and designs they ended up with. They took on a more sachlich approach to architecture, basing their design on hard and clear realities of architectural production, no longer directly engaging themselves in the construction of grand narrative or group activities. Acknowledging the irreversibility of the process of individualization and the secularization of values in architecture and Korean society at large, they were no longer the prolific writers their seniors once were, and chose to speak through their designs, in languages inherent to the discipline, such as form, space, programming, materiality, and tectonics.

Certain common experiences fueled this change of attitude: born in the 1960s, they were the first generation to benefit from the military regime's international open-door policy of the late 1980s to pursue their post-graduate studies abroad. Many went on to study in the United States and Europe at prestigious academies, and furthermore, they extended their stay to gain professional experience overseas, many under internationally renowned architects such as Rem Koolhass, Steven Holl, Zaha Hadid, Ito Toyo, and Alvaro Siza. These foreign experiences exposed them to systematic pedagogy that Korean universities had yet to establish, and then to new modes and methodologies of practice, and broader cultural implications and higher technical standards of architectural production. There was also a certain change in the cultural scene in general: gradually reaching the end of the twentieth century, with post-fascist ideals of individual freedom reaching the very core of the creative minds, new trends could be observed in other cultural spheres such as art, literature, and music. In particular, parallel movements can be found in the realm of motion pictures, another capital-concentrated medium realized through collaborative process. A new generation of young filmmakers emerged with works that were thematically diverse, technically proficient, realistic in depiction and experimental in form. They moved away from the didactic themes and theatricality of then current Korean cinema, producing visceral films that celebrated cinema's own capacity to communi-

cate on multiple levels, and soon caught the attention of international critics and audiences. The fact that many of these filmmakers commissioned the emerging architects to design their offices and residences speaks of their kindred spirits.

An external factor of change was the financial crisis of 1997 that forced the nation to accept IMF aid and reform conditionalities. With the majority of building projects cancelled or postponed the construction industry came to a halt, and even after the economy recovered in the early 2000s, the career of many senior architects never really recovered from this time of recession, as they were deemed old school all of a sudden in a reformed society. The younger generation, in comparison, quickly became active as they successfully tapped into the demands of the new millennium, marking a clear shift of generations.

As much as they share the zeal for a new beginning, freeing themselves from preconceived conceptual frameworks of the past, the directions these young architects took from this autonomous starting point are startlingly diverse. Compared to their immediate seniors, no singular frame of thought or formal style could be found among them: for example, minimalist constraints in composition, color, and materiality found in the works by Kim Jong-kyu or Choi Wook cannot be more different from the Surrealist-inspired and often kitsch works by Moon Hoon (one of his projects is titled Two Moon Junction, for those who know '80s sleaze cinema), as are Cho Min-suk's deliberately incongruous juxtapositions of diverse and even opposing formal languages, questioning the traditional ideal of integration in an age of much more complex architectural and urban circumstances. Furthermore, there are those who display no consistent formal traits: those such as Choi Moon-gyu have relinquished their role as form-givers, redefining the profession as an arbitrator of given conditions for architectural production (site, context, program, budget, client, collaborators, regulations), emphasizing the analytical, project-specific process of design over form, and thus possessing no particular formal characteristics.[5]

Such diversity of ideas and methods, based on an autonomous approach to the discipline finally free from burdens of identity search and collective social engagement, immediately characterized them against their senior generation of architects, challenging the formal, spatial, programmatic, and structural conventions of Korean architecture, and the new millennium saw their activities in full blossom.

3

Now almost two decades into the twenty-first century—and having gone through another financial crisis in 2008, this time not limited to the nation but global in scale—there is also an even younger groups of architects, whose shared modes of practice define another generation. Setting up their own firms much earlier than their predecessors, many in their early 30s age-wise, they usually work as partnerships in much broader fields of practice, including not only the design of buildings but art installation, exhibition design, book or web publication, real estate consultant, and academic research, unhindered by previous conventions of practice. In an age of low economic growth, they are swiftly responding to the emergence of a new market of young clients and their small-scale yet diverse, interdisciplinary commissions. Among this publication's subjects JOHO Architecture and L'EAU Design could be classified as forerunners of this generation, and while the newcomers are perhaps yet too young to gain wide recognition, they add to the wide spectrum of generations in coexistence that generate the colorful dynamics of the current architectural landscape in Korea. [6]

All in all, it is now quite apparent that there is almost no hint of a pursuit for collectivity in Korean architecture, be it in the form of group efforts or the construction of a grand narrative such as national identity. This is arguably quite in contrast to Japan, which, as has been displayed at 'A Japanese Constellation' show at MoMA (2016), has a clearer self-recognition of creative lineage, and relates its ancient and modern architectural heritage to the construction of a national image, as exemplified in Mori Art Museum's recent ambitious exhibition 'Japan in Architecture' (2018). However, it is important to note that this does not connote that Korean contemporary architects relinquished the project of representation altogether. Their refusal to engage in direct conversations on the issue of modernizing tradition does not entail that their works are void of regional features. Rather, their idea of regionality is not based on a priori conceptual framework, as was in the past decades, but on clear and present realities of architectural production.

And in Korea this reality is always complex, contradictory, and in constant fluctuation: this intensely urbanized nation (Seoul being one of the densest megalopolises of the world) is known for its swift cycles of development and redevelopment, backed by a culture prone to sudden changes of fashion. Its natural conditions are also challenging, with mountainous geography and extremely varying weather conditions across four seasons. Added to these are the realities of the building industry: (limited) availability of materials and construction technology, building codes, bureaucratic requirements, and the peculiar relationships with clients and collaborators.

Through a sober, unbiased, objective approach to these realistic situations, a unique, multi-faceted character was born. Working with challenging ruptures between program and site, density and time, material and capital, or any other combination resulting from complex realities, their works feature shared characteristics of skillful mediating of conflicts, through their own choice of agendas and architectural languages. This diversity of interests and styles, coming from the experience and knowledge of multiple generations, has enriched the contemporary landscape of built environment in Korea, and in extension inspires the world at large, which, in an age of prolonged stagnation under the shadows of globalization, is in need of models more sensitive and responsive to its regional conditions.

[1] Jeon Bong-hee, "A Living History: Launching the Oral History Series on Modern Architects", Kim Jung-sik Oral History (Seoul: Mati. 2011), p.6.

[2] In a nation that has undergone fast-track economic development, the self-awareness of the highly condensed process of modernization, that we may have skipped a few development phases critical in the history of Western advanced countries, was quite strong. In the architectural community, such sense of anxiety was somewhat relieved in the final year of the twentieth century, which saw the completion of SK Headquarters, a quintessential modernist work designed by Kimm Jong-soung, a disciple of Mies van der Rohe.

[3] There had been much controversy when the participants for the Korean Pavilion at the 2012 Venice Architecture Biennale were comprised of CEOs of large design firms, diverting from the usual choice of those who lead independent practices. However, the customary distinction between corporate firm and the so-called atelier-type practice still needs to be reassessed in Korea, since, as late as the late 1980s, it was the former that was known for innovative design.

[4] 4.3 Group today is mostly remembered by its sole exhibition "Echoes of an Era", held at Ingong Gallery in December 1992, and its accompanying publication of the same name (Seoul: Ahn Graphics, 1992), both featuring highly original formal experiments. Their legacy has been a subject of historical reevaluation in Pai Hyung-min, et al., 4.3 Group and the Transitional Period of Korean Architecture (Seoul: Zip, 2014).

[5] A further elaborated introduction on several key figures of this generation is presented in Choi Won-joon, "Sections of Autonomy: Six Korean Architects", Luca Galofaro, ed., Sections of Autonomy: Six Korean Architects (Melfi: Libria, 2017), pp.8-20.

[6] The first magazine feature devoted to this generation of architects was "Emergence of Groups of Architects Born in the 1980s", Space 612 (November 2018), pp.44-131.

Contents

The Condition of Seoul Architecture

by Pier Alessio Rizzardi

FAR
Winning the Game

Seoul
Schizophrenic City

"Rough"
Fighting 'The Roof on the Glass Box'

K-Pop-Arch
Constant Ephemeral Culture

2008 Crisis
Client Renaissance

FAR
Winning the Game

Seoul grew rapidly: 1.6 million inhabitants in 1955, 3.5 million in 1965, 8.4 million in 1984, and more than 10 in 1990. Now they are over 25 million. If we consider the most extreme cities for density and population around the world, Seoul is second only next to Mumbai and Lagos. Moreover, Seoul occupies 12% of the nation's land but is where half of the population lives.

The exodus of migration from the countryside began 50 years ago. After the Korean war, the city saw the cost of land increased by 680 times, reaching $80,000 per square meter in central areas. In this situation, ROI, return on the investment, becomes the watchword that influences development. The current situation is the result of a long period began in the 60s in which Laissez-faire and illegal development heavily influenced today's building landscape. To counteract authorized constructions, the government has imposed very strict and restrictive laws for developers, limiting the building volumes and seriously skyrocketed the real estate market. With rising land prices, clients want to exploit the building envelope to the fore. Until recently, multi-family houses and mixed-use buildings were designed by technicians and surveyors. They were considered too low-class architecture to involve medium-sized companies or ateliers. After the crisis of 2008, the scarcity of square meters pushed clients to turn to the ingenuity of the ateliers, the only ones capable of making the impossible, finding creative solutions that magically multiply the available floor area.

If on one hand, ateliers have more possibilities to build, on the other hand they've become victims of the system, strangled by the volumetric demands of the clients and by a strong building regulation, where the new concepts and discourses seem to have little room to play with. Building codes impose strict diagonal limits starting from setbacks, roads, and existing buildings. The results are a particular conformation of Korean buildings, where the combination of these lines forms pyramidal shells that architects must follow to build the maximum volume.

On an urban scale, the coded architecture negatively affects public and semi-public spaces. Legally, empty spaces like courtyards, terraces, or entrances are considered part of the volume. For architects, it means limiting empty spaces to a minimum to satisfy volume maximization.

To win the FAR game, architects use strategies such as:
- Planimetric-Tactics that make the most of every square meter, reducing corridors and lengthening balconies and terraces;
- Volumetric-Tactics that extend the architecture volumes to the limit of the building envelope, following the exact shape given by the code.
- Cross-sectional-Tactics that reduce the floor heights to obtain more levels, also using basements and habitable attics.

In 2016, the exhibition of the Korean Pavilion at the Venice Biennale entitled "FAR Game" has internationally brought the issues to light that characterize the work of Korean architects; where the situation is so severe that when a building is built, it risks being demolished immediately to make room for a potentially more profitable building, satisfying the ROI rules.

In practice, clients ask for projects that can be designed and built in just a few weeks. Used to the possibilities before the crisis and driven by international references, they demand unique and innovative buildings. From Intellectual architects' figure of the past, able to generate discourse and trends, they assume the role of a mere mediator of the condition, making sure to deliver on time. An architecture in which everything is well-thought and refined becomes impossible, but still aspiring to fame, architects inevitably have to find ingenious solutions, experiment and innovate, focusing on specific details or perhaps part of the facade, which would be manageable and relatively inexpensive elements that can create a greater aesthetic or refined impact on the overall image of the architecture.

Using ingenious new conceptual and constructive solutions, sometimes they are at the forefront in the world; they test new construction processes never tried before, modular prototype form-works, reinforced plastic, vacuum forming, and quick assembly modules, with which they can survive the Korean market and at the same time push the discipline forward.

Thanks to the strong presence of the FAR game, a new and unpredictable environment is emerging, which is not only laying the foundations for a new future coherent context but also a tangible impact on international architectural discourse.

The Scale of Repetition
Photo by Photo by Jennifer
Bailey

14

The Constant Presence
Photo by author

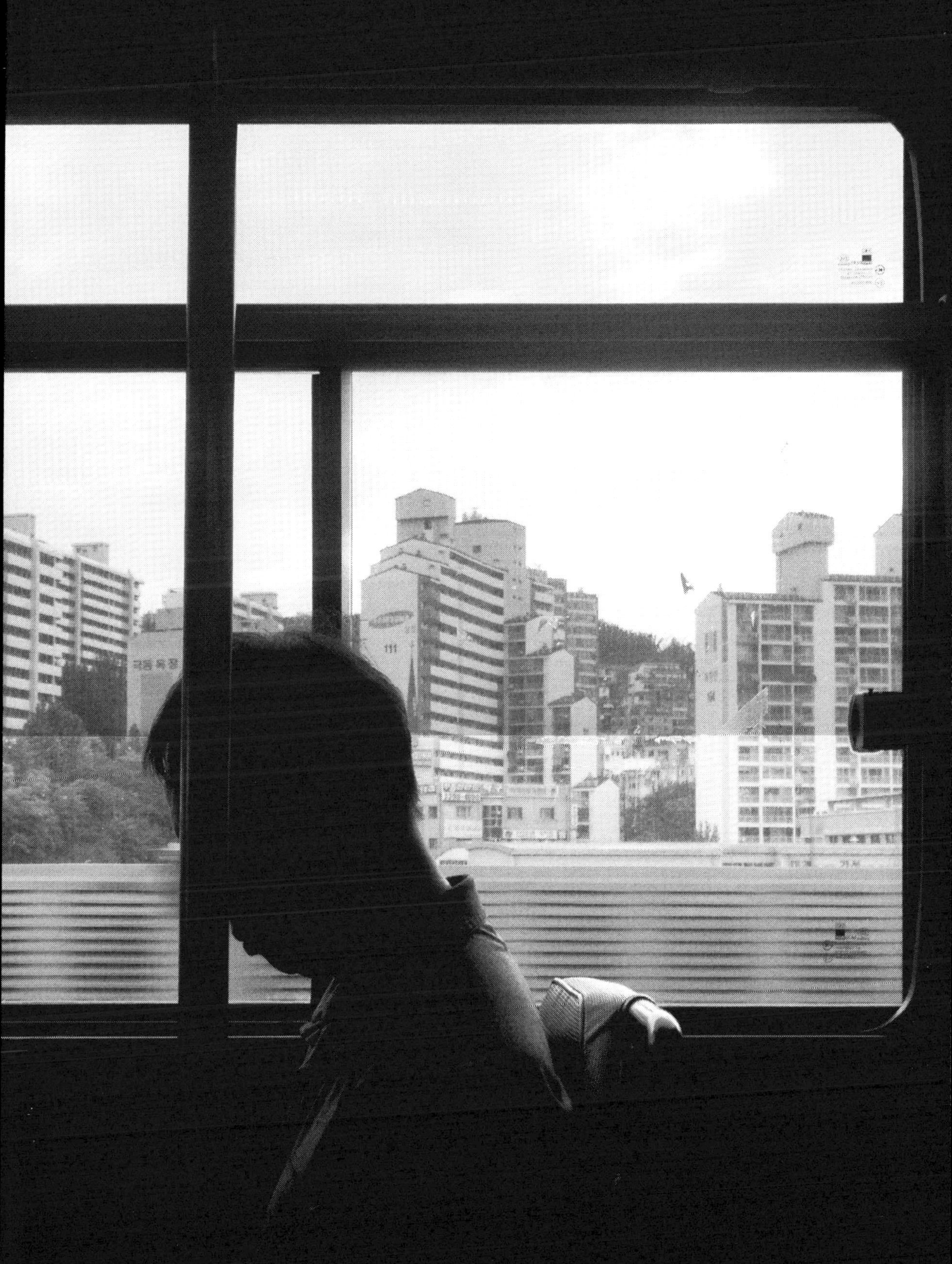

Traces of and the Old Future
Photo by author

Residential Mass Production
Photo by the author

Real Estate with the "Hat"
Photo by Jennifer Bailey

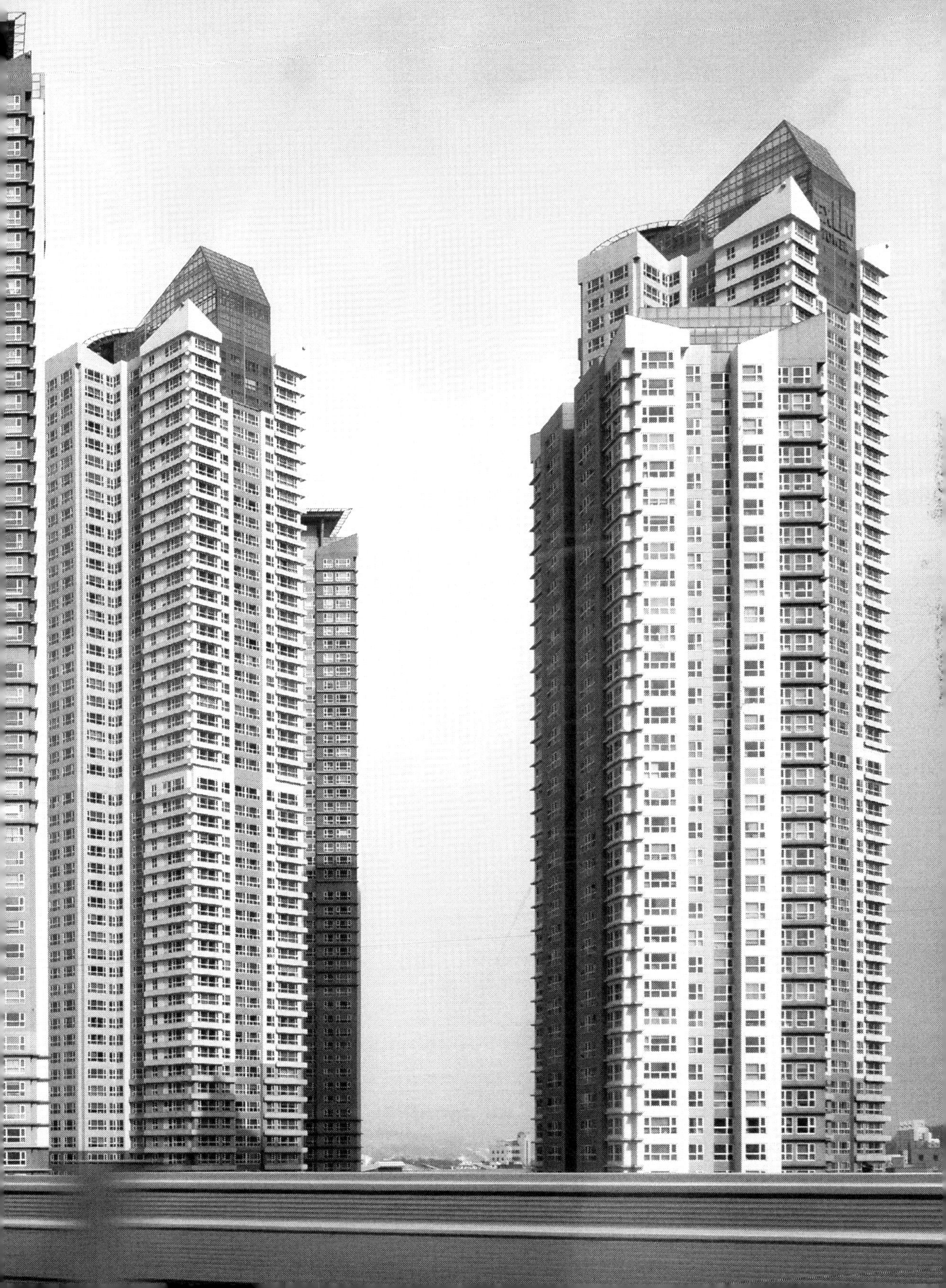

Left
Patchwork City
Photo by Jennifer Bailey

Right top
Impossible Scale
Photo by the author

Right bottom
The FAR Game
Photo by Francisco Anzola

The Schizophrenic City
Photo by author

This and previous page
The Contrast City
Photo by author

Seoul
Schizophrenic City

The Schizophrenic City
Photos by the author

Seoul has a schizophrenic urban fabric in which architects can hardly apply contextualist ideals learned abroad.

There are old and new cities within the city of Seoul: the city of hills, the international city, the city of the rich, the city of alcohol, the city of entertainment, the city of corruption and the city of tourists. On the same block, parts built 600 years ago and in the 19th century could be seen together with others built only ten years ago. The urban landscape is a collection of real and virtual places, natural and artificial, high and low density, highrise and lowrise, where the new degraded and irregular areas compete for the spotlight with shopping-center machines, destroying the delicate urban structure that has been maintained for generations.

Everything can change in a very short time, and temporality, plurality, irregularity, dispersion, inconsistency, and a-hierarchy are constant features of the urban fabric of Seoul. The architects admire the historical layering of the cities where they have studied and visited and appreciate the qualities of commingling and harmony of the different eras. Instead, the old tiny *Hanok* areas, the buildings of the beginning of the last century, and other small buildings designed by the ateliers are flooded by real estate developments, megastructures, and skyscrapers, creating no evident historical layers. Until a few years ago, the main objective was modernization, and there was no widespread criticism; but now Seoul has reached a condition of contradiction in the very definition of the Western context, dividing the local architects between heroic-critics and post-critical pragmatists.

Throughout the history of the last 60 years, in Japan, generations of architects have had continuous and congruous cultural growth. Since the end of the Second World War, the society has had a careful examination of its traditional and cultural characteristics through international parameters. The results were mainly by the incisive Japanese architecture which was deeply rooted in international discourse. Korea has tried to follow the same path, but the results have been plurilateral and contradictory.

To understand the current condition in Korea, we must observe the most prolific and representative architects active today in Seoul. In this heterogeneous group, we can distinguish main age groups in their 60s, 50s, and 40s. Belonging to different historical, political, and economic periods, they share different values and are the authors of a highly diversified production.

The architects in their 60s are independent experimental designers. They started working under the influence of Kim Swoo-geun and learned from his specific interpretation of tradition, creating spontaneous architectures and experimentations, linked to the international revolutionary trends of the early 50s. Being close to the ideas of 4.3 Group, they avoid both the reproduction of the traditional style and the postmodern pastiche, but reinterpret the philosophical qualities of Korean art. Their purpose is to create a universal architecture that deviates from local discourses, trying to reconnect to the international scene. During their careers, they've reached the milestone of personal independence from the identity debate and real estate dynamics.

The architects in their 50s are the first to study abroad and gain first-hand experience of the international culture. Big investors see the potential and let them design the most important buildings with extensive freedom to express themselves. These are the people who have had a double-culture shock; first when they went abroad to study a different design methodology, and second when they returned, finding themselves in an alienated situation from a context they understood and in which they learned to design. Through these shocks, they have become tough thinkers, able to re-discuss the dogmas of the discipline and to find unique design philosophies.

The architects, in their 40s, took their first steps during the economic crisis. Being the second generation who studied abroad, the novelty of the international experience was no longer sufficient to have the possibilities of the previous generation. At the same time, they were hit by a severe economic crisis, where their attention was attracted entirely by the economic aspects and the speed of construction. They are active investigators of cutting-edge technologies, time-saving solutions, cost-effective materials, and prefabrication strategies. They try to be active worldwide, participating in international exhibitions and visiting the Biennales and Design Weeks to tap into the new ideas of the avant-garde. They do not participate in the debate of identity and speak very little of tradition, but with their production strive to create an impact, and gain fame at a national and international level.

Although the architects-in-their-40s are the most experimental and prolific, they are still in the shadow of those in their 50s and 60s, still considered the representatives of standard Korean characters. However, we are now observing a new period of transition, shifting the discussion to an international level and deeply aware of identity, cultural, economic, and social issues.

"Rough"
Fighting 'The Roof on the Glass Box'

The Beauty of Rough
Photos by the author

Kim Swoo-geun died in 1986, leaving the young architects in a state of disorientation, and period of cultural and ideological confusion.
In the 80s, many of the identity solutions were based on direct use of the concept 'The Roof on the Glass Box'.
The desire to find an alternative Korean native character led them to reflect on the cultural difference between Korea and its neighbors: China, and Japan. In the early 1990s, a group of young architects gathered under the name of 4.3 Group, to form the only Korean architectural movement with the names of: Kwak Jae-Hwan; Kim Byung-Yoon; Kim In-Cheurl; Do Chang-Hwan (Aka Do-Gaag); Dong Jung-Kuen; Min Hyun-Sik (Kiohun); Bang Chul-Lin; Baek Moon-Ki; Seung H-Sang; Woo Kyung-Kook (Yegong); Lee Sung-Kwan (Hanul); Lee Il-Hoon; Lee Jong-Sang; Joh Sung-Yong.
Through various congresses and publications, they have laid the foundations for an attempt to resume the debate on architecture. Their interest was to study and document the ancient artifacts; they spoke of origins, principles of beauty and, above all, the concept of "rough" to be used in

contemporary architecture.
In medieval China and Japan, beauty was seen as the appreciation of precision and elegance. The artifacts of the same period, exhibited at the Leeum Museum, show a different way of perceiving beauty in Korea. The ceramics of the Chosum Dynasty (1392-1897), are defined by imperfections and irregularities, originating from hands movements and brushes left during the creation process. In the same collection, the shape of the Moon Jar shows how at first sight it is composed of two elements joined together in the middle, which naturally adapt to each other during the cooking process.
The intelligentsia appreciated the energy imprinted on the surfaces of materials, coming from the passage of time and exposure of the elements. To do so, they avoid any decoration and use raw, pure, and uncoated materials, able to show textures and natural appearances.
Receiving both a cultural status and greater freedom of expression, both critical and pragmatic architects apply the "rough" tool, in some cases in a comprehensive way and sometimes only timidly, genuinely adding value to the design.

K-Pop-Arch
Constant Ephemeral Culture

"K-Pop Arch"
1. CC0 Public Domain
2-3-4-8. Photos by the author
5-6-7. Photo by Aleksander Zykov

The Korean peninsula is located in a strategic position that has led to a history influenced by crises, wars, occupations, dictatorships, closures, openings, and foreign influences, setting the bases for a constant ephemeral condition. Traditionally, there has always been a cultural structure in which literature, art, and architecture were at very high levels, but after each upheaval, there was a consequent long static period to reinstate the previous standards. With wars and occupations, the urban fabric has undergone numerous demolitions and reconstructions, and along with it, culture has been repeatedly reestablished; first during the different Japanese wars and invasions, and then with American influence, undergoing physical and cultural reconstructions. After the Korean war, everything was erased, leading to a severe economic and cultural recession. In a climate of constant change, people pragmatically adapt to a survival philosophy of life.

The military dictatorship of the 60s found fertile ground supported by the logic of the Cold War against Northern Communism. The new state led to a time that aimed at capitalist development and the rapid change of society, leading to a culture of *"pali-pali"* [Hurry up!], also triggering the spark of the process that today is identified as K-Pop.

Until the 80s, people were not allowed to travel abroad, but this changes with the 1988 Olympics. People started to go abroad to study and work, bringing their experience back home. In the 90s, the ruling class is substituted by foreign-experienced youth, who began to look at architecture with interest, starting to shift attention to a particular spatial and cultural quality.

In 2002, the World Cup arrived in Korea, creating new positive energy, transforming the face of the nation. Driven by this spirit, society begins to change, which started an era of new technological optimism, stimulating the environment with possible future opportunities.

All the great changes suffered by Korea in the last century have produced a pragmatic society open to new international ideas and always in search of new and fashionable trends, pushing people to use creative resources to find possibilities in the constant ephemeral condition.

Until recently, Koreans had imported a large part of art, music, and films from the west, Japan and Hong Kong. As the masses embraced the novelty, the Korean intelligentsia immediately saw the pop-capitalist-movement as an impoverishment of culture. They feared a flattening of culture, bringing a national identity crisis.

In the early 2000s, we see how the situation is reversed. As a culture importer, Korea has become an exporter of films, music, and soap operas to Asia, Japan, and Hong Kong. Korean Pop Culture becomes one of the emerging cultures, influencing the international community with efficient communicators. K-pop [Korean pop music], a term derived from the musical genre, is now making its way to become a relevant creative form, which draws from communication to the mass and is becoming the distinctive trait par excellence that characterizes every commercial or artistic production, from art to business, to music, soap operas and films.

The latest generation of architects are the representatives of this trend, building an instant, efficient, and highly communicative architecture. Many of them do not require any theoretical explanation and can be directly assimilated by the masses. Architects like Moon Hoon do not explain architecture in theoretical or historical terms, but through a common language that entertains and creates the show.

Thus the K-Pop Architects create an architecture that can be brought to the common people by bridging the gap between society and architecture.

2008 Crisis
Client Renaissance

1. **Hundai Development Corporation Headquarter**
Photo by Aleksander Zykov
2. **Dongdaemun Design Plaza**
Public Domain
3. **Leeum Museum**
Photo by Sun Kwon-yu
4. **Mario Botta**
Photo by the author
5. **Seoul University Museum of Art**
Photo by Forgemind Archimedia
6. **Ehwa Womans University**
Photo by Park Nam-ho
7. **Jongro Millennium Tower**
Photos by the author
8. **Incheon Tri-Bowl**
Public Domain

In the past, the architecture of the important projects leaned towards big names in the international scene such as Zaha Hadid, OMA or Jean Nouvel. The situation has left local small and medium-sized studios outside, giving the possibility only to large companies to design and excel, and the ateliers was under a lethargic state for more than a decade.

From the first decade of the 2000s, we see how the intelligentsia, followed by society, began to criticize the work of the Archistars. Their projects were considered extraneous to the Korean situation and as insignificant objects superimposed onto the urban landscape. It is believed that foreigners were not able to understand the local situation and the sin in relating too much to the visible chaotic contemporary city and not with the historical or cultural heritage.

During the lethargic moment, the ateliers taught in the main Korean universities, strengthening their resistance and culture, with the research and development of new architectural concepts and the production of numerous design competitions. However, with the economic crisis of 2008, the situation changes; archistars took a step back, and the small studios received the opportunity to build.

The "post-2008 generation" is the one that no longer has access to easily earned opportunities. The crisis and taxes have paralyzed the market, and the government has tightened the building regulations, limiting the land exploitation. To attract tenants and buyers, customers look for interesting and communicative solutions and with intelligent use of square meters; something "k-pop" that they have never seen before. Now, the clients have changed and appreciated the creativity of the ateliers, which also pays in economic terms. From the harsh situation, architects have finally the opportunity to realize their agendas thanks to a crisis that stimulates a new Korean renaissance of the clients.

Contingent Topographies

by John Hong

Korea is nearly two-thirds mountainous. Diverse and often stunning precipices, valleys, and waterways form its topography. While ancient geomantic principles once governed patterns of human settlement, urbanization in Korea, especially in the last half century, has witnessed a hybridization of the existential materials of landscape and city. But even as Korea's capital Seoul became the second densest metropolis in the world surpassing New York by two times, its image did not take on the latter's iconic high-rise buildings, but instead entangled with hillsides and riverfronts.

In this way, this writing is not about the inherent nostalgia embedded within the discussion of ancient and modern, nature and urban. Instead, it is about an emerging body of work that altogether eschews the subtext of what has been 'lost' when city and topography enmesh. Korean architects such as Seunghoy Kim of KYWC, Yerin Kang and Chi Hoon Lee of SoA, and Minsuk Cho of Mass Studies, are translating the topographic condition in specific and notable ways with a 'no-regrets' view toward existing conditions. While it is true that grounds have been scraped away and ecosystems degraded by reified development

and massive layers of infrastructure, their body of work is less an apologetic atonement for an unrecoverable past, but an alchemic synthesis born from the often unwieldy coordination of program, politics, cultural concerns, and harrowing economic and legal limitations. Topography therefore becomes the medium through which an expanded sense of the collective permeates through their projects' boundaries. The previously assumed dichotomy between 'nature and artifice,' 'figure and ground,' lose their significance. Of the three works that will be discussed, Youngdong Church by KYWC, is the only thus far built example. It was selected for the way it succinctly represents what is possible in negotiating the physical and cultural aspects of topographic architecture. The two other works, Four Round Tables: Sang-Saeng Village Community Center and Parking Garage by SoA and Danginri Podium and Promenade by Mass Studies, are intentionally chosen as unbuilt (but soon to be completed examples) because of the way they point toward the compelling future role of topographic architecture in building multiple contingencies between a site's social, cultural, and ecological context.

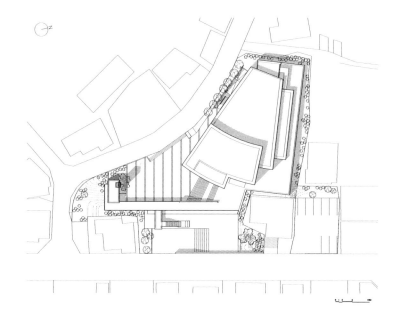

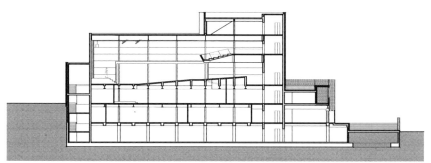

Youngdong Church
Courtesy of KYWC Architects

Youngdong Church

The forces of capital continue to reify Seoul's urbanscape through 2-dimensional individual lot lines 'printed' onto 3-dimensional terrain. Economies and technologies limit how topography is shaped, with roads and foundations built to the available techniques of their times. Later frozen into legal delimitations, oddly triangular property lines then reinforce and problematize the condition. In this way, negotiating this challenging topography has its own unique significance in the formation of Seoul's urbanism. Beyond the simplified idea of 'ground and building,' in the best-case scenario, topographic architecture can be synthetic, revealing a palimpsest of historical networks. Such is the case with KYWC's Youngdong Church. The design manifests the way topography continues beyond the project's immediate site, extending the building's influence to the underlying pre-existing structures of sloped roads and alleyways. Nestled within a dense and tightly knit community in the Yeungdungpo district, the site is poised between a 7m elevational difference between its front and back roads. Design principal Seunghoy Kim used this as an opportunity to converge the site's networks with the complex community programs of the church. Instead of an enclosed and singularly monumentalized space, three separate floors of the building including cafeteria, educational spaces, and meeting rooms, connect to the surrounding streets on various sides. Circulation from the outside to the inside is increased through carefully planned entrances and glazing that extend the pedestrian flow from adjacent streets and alleyways.

The main gathering space of the church itself however, hovers above the site as an abstract, translucent volume. This condition of 'hovering' is also part of the topographic design strategy: Instead of structure and walls definitively meeting the ground, the urban networks are allowed to flow beneath it.

The worship hall's indeterminacy, amplified by its ghostly skin, represents a kind of anti-monumentality. Because of its elevated status and the site's complex geometry, its volume cannot be understood at once instance. Where a church facade typically contains a flat forecourt plaza to announce its presence, there is no such luxury within the dense topographic city. Instead, we apprehend the building through fragmented glimpses between alleyways. What could be understood as a new kind of 'plaza' is then folded underneath the church as an interior condition. As a precursor to the later projects mentioned in this writing, the Youngdong Church encapsulates four emerging ways in which topography is utilized to generate urban contingency.

1. Topography is integral to the public networks of the city and can be leveraged to generate connections to the surrounding community.

2. Topography extends programmatic influence past the boundaries of the site.

3. Rather than separating nature and urban, it synthesizes and intensifies their relationship.

4. Topography is strategic artifice: It is used to exert a conceptual and functional project goal.

Four Round Tables
Sang-Saeng Village Community Center and Parking Garage

Located in a fallow buffer zone between a mega industrial factory and an older low-rise fine-grain residential area, the bulk of Four Round Tables is essentially a cleverly disguised parking lot buried beneath a series of community, cooking, daycare, and green spaces. There is no mythology naturalizing the programming *vis-à-vis* gently sloped landscapes reclaiming some non-existent past. Instead, the potential smoothness of the slope is translated and abstracted into stepped gardens, circulation paths, and semi-circular roofscapes. In this way, Four Round Tables is a semantic project: its physical reality merges with the abstract language of a contour line drawing. And as a language composed of 'readable' geometries, it allows its users to interpret the topography in ways they see fit: as rest areas, gathering spaces to share a meal, and as functional pathways between living and working. Instead of the 'otherness' of nature versus the city, it is a synthesis of it.

Just as the KYWC Youngdong Church recognizes that topography extends beyond the immediate project site, Four Round Tables also takes on this challenge not only by extending its paths but also through programmatic use at the master planning scale. For instance, the camouflaged parking garage and its rooftop gardens work together to integrate with the patterns of the community's daily life. Through what the architects call 'time geography,' the daily ritual of parking and walking home is blended with community programs of daycare, urban farming, and cooking.

Most importantly, by offering a centrally located overflow of parking spaces, the previous street parking in front of individual homes can be reterritorialized by residents for alternative uses such as pocket green areas. The result is that the vegetated centrality of Four Round Tables becomes a supporting catalyst for the growth of surrounding semi-private green areas dotted throughout the community. Moreover, even though the project is actually a building, it presents itself as a public landscape. This is an important distinction because the connotation is that buildings can be 'owned' while large-scale green spaces 'belong' to the public sphere.

To the point of strategic artificiality, Four Round Tables explicitly deviates from a conventional landscape: Where its stepped garden paths generally approximate the sloped terrain, the programs themselves appear as architectural 'piers' terminating with four semi-circular canopies. The space beneath these overhangs are deep, reef-like undercuts. Through another layer of semantic play, the volume of the canopy from the exterior reads as a thick jutting layer of ground. However, from beneath its volume, we realize that its very thickness is formed by a thin vaulted extrusion. The canopy's dual reading as a modernist cantilever from the exterior or a pre-modern 'grotto' from the interior amplifies it as a hybrid inside/outside zone. Its intentional ambiguity allows the interior life of the programs to intersect with the public activities along the sidewalk.

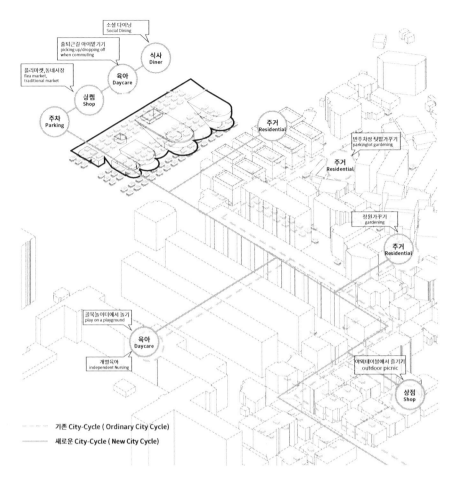

기존 City-Cycle (Ordinary City Cycle)

새로운 City-Cycle (New City Cycle)

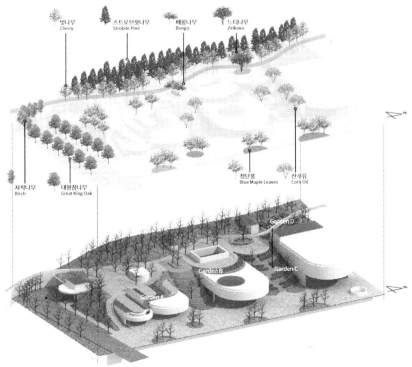

Four Round Tables
Courtesy of SoA

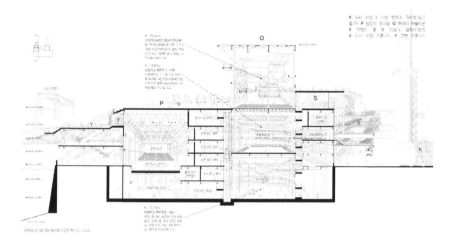

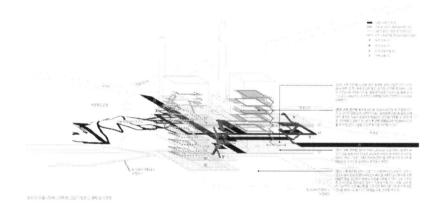

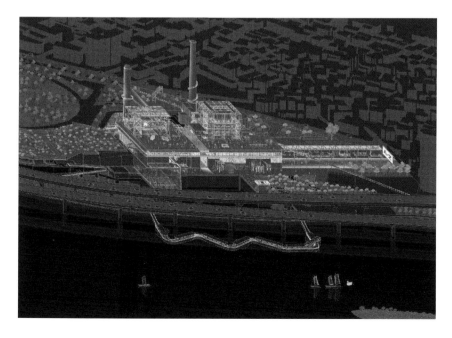

Danginri
Courtesy of Mass Studies

Danginri Podium and Promenade

One of the current urgent quests of the Seoul City Government is the reclamation of waterfronts in response to the previous era's massive infrastructural accretion. However, like conducting open-heart surgery on a patient that is still running a marathon, there is no way to recover an 'original' topographic condition when the city around it has to function continually. Such is the case with the Danginri Podium and Promenade, a public competition won by Minsuk Cho and his firm Mass Studies to turn a defunct power station into a public cultural space. Originally built on the north side of the Han River in the 1930s in the Hapjeongdong district, Seoul's increasing urban growth pressured a parallel demand on its power grid: The massive Danginri power station is the result of five stages of expansion. Similarly, transportation expansion resulted in severing Dangrinri's riverfront access. The successive accumulation rather than one wave of construction became a kind of slow dementia, a typical condition in Seoul where the transformation of the topography in stages erases any notion of an original condition. In the case of Danginri, the waterfront, landscapes, and the factory became intertwined into one industrialized zone.

Recognizing this irreducible entanglement is the strength of Mass Studies' intervention into a complex that originally had no intention of being used as public space. Going back to the analogy of surgery, three axes, like a precise urban-scale needle and thread, interweave existing and new. Named the 'industrial,' ecological,' and 'short cut' streets, they organize diverse programs such as urban farms, wetlands, exhibit, and performance spaces within the framework of the existing power plant and surrounding grounds. Instead of the easy polarization of nature and urban, however, the crossing of these axes create three-dimensional hybrid experiences. Materialized by spiral circulation networks, new programs, new narratives, physical artifacts, and landscapes intertwine. The connections take diverse forms of outside and inside, covered and open, existing, and new. The 'shortcut' road then creates a 'third term' that further destabilizes the binary logics of industry and ecology. Referencing the work of Gordon Matta-Clark, it metaphorically cuts through the landscape and industrial artifacts before leading to the waterfront, acting as an alternative promenade that allows one to gain a critical distance from the immersive project.

However, the stark reality of the Gangbyun elevated expressway along the waterfront is a physical impasse that narrative alone cannot overcome. A counterpoint to their nuanced promenade strategy, Mass Studies constituted a bold directness by reclaiming the roof of the power station as a massive public podium. Hovering 17m above the existing grade, this elevated topography will afford views over (and through) the columns of the expressway. In what can only be understood as a 'fight-fire-with-fire' strategy, its horizontal monumentality matches up against the monumentality of the expressway itself. Unlike other roof decks where one has to enter the building to reach it, however, the podium is accessible without ever having to enter the building. Therefore, the interior is never positioned as a method of control. This 'exteriority' of the podium is amplified by the fact that food-trucks and large objects can be brought up to this deck. Rather than interpreting the roof as a rarified garden, the podium is a more rough-and-ready space with a built-in durability that gains value the more it is used.

The concept that topography extends beyond the site boundary gives the public space of Danginri resiliency by the simple fact that it is contingent to other urban spaces. In the act of sheer providence, several years prior, Mass Studies also won the invited competition for the Bamseom Ecological Observation Deck directly south of the power plant. The project takes the highly compromised infrastructural waterfront and creates a dynamically transforming habitat and floating walkway. As the original landscape was destroyed, the new design acknowledges the constant reciprocity between human-made and natural forces. Mass Studies' solution of 'floating beams' does not naturalize the landscape, but rather blends with the linearity of the highways. They act as another infrastructure, this time ecological, that protects habitat of sedimentary mounds that will continue to change with tidal conditions.

Therefore, we come to the 4th point of topography: that it is a strategic and self-aware mechanism rather than a passive acceptance of nature. The coordination of Danginri's urban section is an inseparable hybrid between nature and artifice, decks and ground, artifacts and atmospheres. They resist congealing into a whole but instead remain an assembly of fragments. The importance of conceptualizing topography as contingent instances is that they can represent a diverse public realm outside of a singular controlling entity.

Topographic Contingencies

"The City of Hills"
1-6. Photos by the author
7-9. Photos by Aleksandr Zykov

Richard Rorty in his still seminal and controversial book, Contingency, Irony and Solidarity, rejects the idea of "self-subsistent facts" that are thought to precede language. Instead of capitalizing the word "truth" he would rather treat reality as contingent, that is gaining meaning as language gains meaning: through relationships with other ideas. In this light he claims, "Solidarity is not discovered by reflection, but created... That recognition would be part of a general turn against theory and toward narrative." Through the morass that 'progress' has left on Korea's urbanscape, a unique 'post-developmental' attitude is emerging within a new body of work. Where on one hand vexing limitations continue to generate projects that merely react to the existing conditions of slopes, streets, infrastructure, and building codes, the synthetic thinking seen in projects by KYWC, SoA, Mass Studies, and other contemporary architects featured in this book are at once systematically typological as well as subjectively narrative. Their solutions do not uncover an idealized 'truth' of pre-existing conditions, but rather focus on idealizing the existing condition in and of itself: This is a subtle but powerful syntactical shift and working mode. It is a palimpsest-like methodology of overlaying historical traces and yet-to-determined future uses.

In this way, the topographic project in Korea converges the entanglement of landscape and architecture with the emerging notions of the democratic city. The above projects shift away from the idea that there is an original (and didactic) site condition. Instead, they wield topography to strategically generate an idea of public space that literally and metaphorically presents multiple entry points for a diverse citizen-body. The irony embedded in the contingent project is that the more public it becomes the less singular and whole its architecture has to be. Because topography inherently compels movement, circulation takes on a new agency as a collector of multiple narratives. In this regard, topographic architecture is always adjusting, multiplying choices, and never congealing into a single reference or vanishing point.

Gangnam Public Realm
at the Feet of the Hill
Photo by the author

Architecture of Cultural Transfers

by Caroline Maniaque Benton

Right page
Representative architecture of the interviewed architects
As credited in the next pages

Next page
Interviews images of the architect
Photo by the author

As an aid to understand the ways in which two cultures can influence, interfere with or contaminate each other, two concepts can be of assistance: that of *"passeurs"*, and that of *"transferts culturels"*(cultural transfers), where the *"passeurs"* serve as the agents of *"transferts culturels"*.[1] The *"passeur"* is usually thought as somebody who passes an obstacle, such as a river, enabling others to cross over afterwards. We find *"passeurs"* throughout the history of art, enabling the passage of ideas and techniques in all the branches of humanity.[2]

Between 1975 and 2000, many hundreds of Korean architects chose to complete their studies in Europe, Japan or the United States. It seemed to them that being a fully rounded architect requires international experience and a good understanding of the story of western architecture. It had been difficult to obtain permission to leave the country before 1988 due to the political regime. Following the stage of the Olympic Games in 1988, however, a democratic regime replaced the military dictatorship.

Kim Young-Joon was one of these Korean architects, who had spent ten years in Europe. He noted: "In the 1970s and 1980s, architecture was considered an industry. After 1988, after the Olympic Games, architecture became culture. Not any more an industrial product but a cultural thing."[3] Without this shift in political outlook, the experience of these Korean architects abroad would have had less impact.

Some architects chose the Architectural Association in England, under the liberal and creative directorship of Alvin Boyardsky. Others went to Italy, attracted by the reputation of the Istituto Universitario di Architettura di Venezia (IUAV), where Giuseppe Samonà, Vittorio Gregotti, Manfredo Tafuri, Carlo Scarpa and Aldo Rossi had established their international reputation. Yet others enrolled in the program initiated by Hermann Hertzberger at the Berlage Institute in Amsterdam. Several others chose Paris, often attracted by the pedagogical reputation of Henri Ciriani at Paris-Belleville. Most of them were already qualified architects, aiming to add a European post- graduate qualification, including, in some cases, a doctorate[4] . Some went as well to the United States, at the University of Michigan, Harvard University and Columbia University.

Many of the Korean architects who have spent

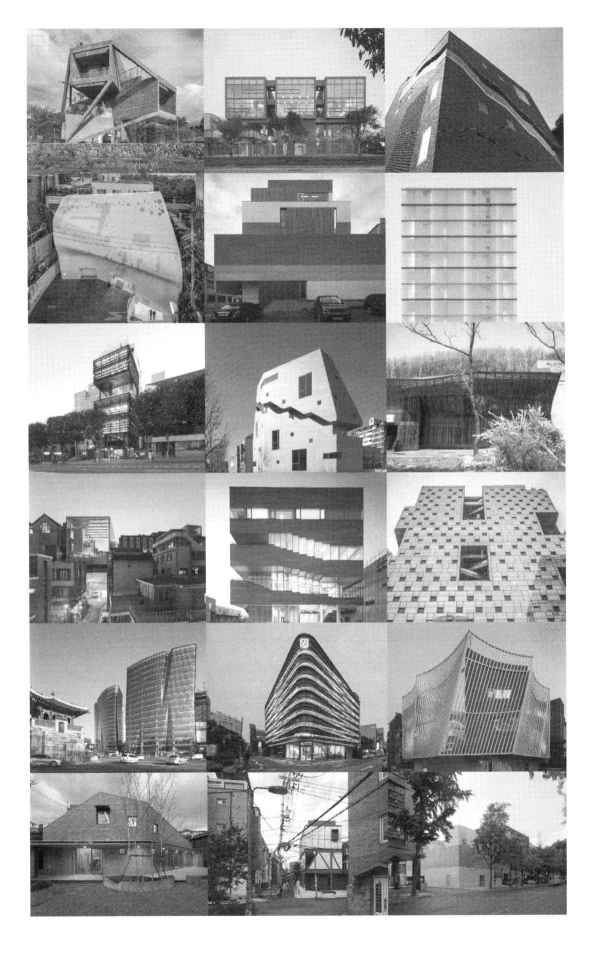

time in Europe, Japan, or North America can now be seen to have been dynamic *"passeurs"*. As a channel of communication, they encouraged others to follow them, creating networks of support and ensuring communications, while working competently in partnership with foreign architects in Korea.

Kim Young-Joon made use of his period in Europe from 1994 to 1997 to develop a considerable network of professional contacts. His impressive address book enabled him to invite distinguished international architects to contribute to the urban development of Paju Book City, dedicated to the publishing industries. These contacts, together with his mastery of English, have enabled him to enter international competitions in partnership with European architects.

Some of the Korean architects also invited their European professors to give lectures or hold workshops in Korea, for example, Renzo Piano, Yves Lion, Florian Beigel, and Francesco Venezia – which led these architects to have successfully built in Korea.

Many of them used their time in Europe or America to write articles on European and North American architecture for Korean publications, thus not only deepening their understanding, but also getting the chance to meet leading architects and visit their studios[5] .The translation of important European texts, such as Jacques Lucan's book on French architecture[6] , provided the necessary tools for their compatriots to better understand European architecture. All this constitutes the network of transfers, exchanges and collaborations between Europe and Korea.

Think about how cultural transfer enables an understanding of some of the ways that American, Japanese, European and Korean experience can be compared. For example, the fact that European projects, typically coming to fruition slowly, contrasts with the sometimes rushed dynamism of Korean constructions.[7] In the interviews carried out in December 2013 and in July 2017, many Korean architects remarked on the contrast between the dynamic growth of a country in which architects were seeing their buildings from the 1970s and 1980s already being demolished and the relative deliberation of Europe in the process of urban change. The geographer Valérie Gelézeau noted as early as 2003, that the residential stock of the city of Seoul had been so radically transformed over the previous forty years, that by 2000, only less than 5% of the city dwellings was built before 1960.

"As for the remains of Seoul dating back before the Korean War (1950-53), they are extremely rare because only 3 % of the existing dwellings from that period have survived."[8]

Many Korean architects were therefore sensitized to the question of permanence, and it is worth noting that the question of urban context was a feature of architectural pedagogy in Paris and Venice in the 1980s. One of the architects remembered Fernando Montes's statement:

"You must pay your respects to the neighboring building."[9]

The juxtaposition of the contemporary with the vernacular is a feature of the Keepers Institute designed by the architect Jong-Kyu Kim. Situated just opposite the presidential palace in Jongro-gu district, this institute aims to promote traditional culture: clothing, pottery, music. On a 320 m2 site, the complex is exquisitely detailed with the use of smooth concrete, red cedar wood and translucent glass. The building extends over several floors, descending at the rear to expose an existing earlier wall that was uncovered during construction. The building also includes a reconstruction of a traditional building which could be used for dance and theatrical representations.

Jong-Kyu Kim's M.A.R.U network (Metropolitan Architecture Research Unit) is located in the SeoCho-gu district on the right bank of the river Han. It is organized on three floors on a small concrete building built in the 1990s. Jong-Kyu Kim retains close ties with the office of Florian Beigel in London; even the name of Jong-Kyu Kim's practice demonstrates his affinity with Florian Beigel's Architecture Research Unit (ARU). The two offices have been collaborating regularly, for example on the Heyri Art Valley and in the Paju Book City, where they have contributed three buildings[10] . The urban theory which Beigel and Jong-Kyu Kim have developed since the 1990s employs the metaphor of landscaping.[11] In these ways Jong-Kyu Kim exemplifies the role of the *passeur*.

After obtaining a Bachelor of Science degree (BS) at Yonsei University, Jong-Kyu Kim decided to study at the Architectural Association in London, between 1979 and 1983, when Alvin Boyarsky was in charge:

"He was a kind of person I think who had very free

thinking. At that time, the AA had no system of regulation [...]. It taught you freedom. I was surprised at that because in my university time, you had to enroll in certain subjects to get the degree. But at the Architectural Association there was no limit at all, you just did the project and through the project you could pass or fail. [...] And the way of thinking was free, so architecture is not only architecture, it can be enlarged into neighbour subjects. That kind of thing was the first thing for me to experience somehow."[12]

Combined with this radical freedom, however, was a respect for the past and an insistence that modern architecture had to 'fit in' the existing urban fabric. Jong-Kyu Kim spent more than ten years in England and was able to teach part time at the North London Polytechnic, at the invitation of Florian Beigel, for whom he also worked, before collaborating with him on the Nara Convention Hall competition. Jong-Kyu Kim noted that his time in Europe was not only a period of architectural, urban and landscaping discovery, but also a cultural experience. The English ritual of tea-time, the pleasure of visiting art galleries, intense discussions with friends and the best way to open a bottle of wine were all part of this European acculturation.

Being immersed in the culture of a foreign country forces one to reflect on his own culture and traditions. The architect Wook Choi remarked: *"If you look at the city, it is clear that we are in a severe cultural crisis. If we think of centuries ago, Korea has always had a well-structured Confucian culture. Art, literature, and architecture were at the highest levels. In the last two centuries, due to wars and invasions, it has gone through periods of growth and destruction, reducing critically."[13]*

And he continued:

"For me, the point to connect to is right before the destruction, colonization, and invasion. [...] I want to reestablish the lost culture. In some ways, I imagine a parallel society where these events didn't destroy it - do not misunderstand me, at the same time, I also want to create an architecture closely linked to the contemporary condition. Imagine if our history continued in a fluid and evolving way, what would Korea look like now?"[14]

Wook Choi had already obtained his BA in architecture in 1985 from Hong LK University in Korea before he left for Italy. From 1986 to 1990, he studied at the IUAV, the Istituto universitario di architettura di Venezia, where he learned a new architectural language as well as how to adapt

existing buildings into a new design. For two years, he took a course in restoration. Carlo Scarpa was one of the key figures in this field and many of his projects were situated in Venice : the entrances of the architectural school and of the faculty of philosophy, the Querini Stampalia foundation, Olivetti showroom and the turnstile entrance at the Biennale. All of these Venetian programmes demanded a respect for the architectural heritage, requiring Scarpa to reflect on the passage of time and the integration of old and new.

Wook Choi came to realize that Italian cities are the result "of deliberation, of a consideration across a long historical continuity, whereas the everyday reality in Korea is more impulsive."[15] He was struck by the permanence of urban structures. Venice is the most extraordinary example of continuity in the built environment. It is probable that Aldo Rossi's book, *'L'Architettura della Città'*, published in 1966, had a strong influence on the Korean architects' visit in Italy. It was a manifesto for the rediscovery of the historic city and of the precise understanding of its evolution. But while learning about restoration and urban morphology, Wook Choi also developed his formal analysis. Peter Eisenman taught at Venice in 1996 and introduced to his students the idea of a linguistic system adapted in architecture: buildings are not simply physical objects, but rather artefacts with meaning. It is interesting that Wook Choi used the word "Platonic" to characterize European thoughts.

A visit to one of Wook Choi's most emblematic projects provides an understanding of his principles. The complex in the Gahoe-dong district in the center of Seoul, completed in 2013, consists of a library dedicated to design, a modern art gallery and a traditional *Hanok* house where a 6 x 6 meter prefabricated pavilion by Jean Prouvé was transferred from Brazzaville via Paris. The latter has been adapted for use as a private study. Even if the programme is complex, the architectural scale is modest, combining different levels of public and private access. It is interesting that the pavilion by Prouvé was discretely renovated in the interior, but left untouched, rusting and chipped on the exterior. This is a double play between a modernization of a traditional house and the presentation of the modern as antiquity.

For the architect Jean Son, an important word is "context" which he discovered with the reading of Kenneth Frampton's text on critical regionalism:[16]

"If you look at Modern Seoul, it is a city with no context. The context is almost impossible to define, study, or fall into any categorization. Here the urban landscape is the result of simple repetitions, which cannot bring you to any theory. For example, in Italy, the context exists, it is not very difficult to find and understand it. All cities have a common and visible urban structure that defines them... Since the birth of Modernity and the adoption of Western typologies, we have had an extreme difficulty in understanding the context and finding strategies on how to deal with it."[17]

One of the buildings realized by Jean Son and Min Lee in 2007, the Unmun kindergarten for the city of Gyeong San, shows how the architect tried to create his own context. The religious Buddhist community was anxious to establish a close relationship with the urban community. The building is articulated in five distinct volumes like the fingers of a hand united in the internal space. This is like a forum where the children can meet or pass through from one activity to another. An urban concept lies at the heart of this little building, like a whole city reduced to the scale of the children's environment.

Jean Son joined the architectural school in Venice (IUAV) at the beginning of the 1980s and followed courses in architectural history and theory by Manfredo Tafuri, Franco Rella, Francesco dal Co and Massimo Cacciari. He paid less attention to his design studies and never completed the diploma at Venice. Nevertheless, he did study with the urban theorist and planner Bernardo Secchi in Venice and developed an urban project for Mestre (the industrialized port of Venice) under his tuition.

"I was struck in Venice by the quality of light. The Mediterranean light is very strong. In Korea I had never paid much attention to the quality of natural light; it was in Italy that I understood."[19]

One of Jean Son's key words is 'resistance'. He decided to use brick, as well as concrete, for external surfaces, not only because it weathers well, but also as a metaphor for the survival of buildings.

"For me, it is very important today that the buildings I construct resist. This must not only be a physical and historic resistance, but also mental. For example, concrete has strong physical properties of resistance, but if ideas change, it can be destroyed very easily. Brick is not like that. Perhaps I obtained this idea of the durability of materials in Europe. For me, it's really important."[20]

Once again, we find the themes mentioned by other architects reappearing, and especially the question of the obsolescence of Korean construction. Francesco Venezia, with whom Jean Son worked for several years in Italy, discusses the question of the durability of materials and the survival of buildings:

"Let's have no illusions, sooner or later, all buildings are undone by nature. But some buildings last 1,000 years, some for 150 years and some only last for three. In fact, I believe that most modern buildings are destined to have a life of fifty or sixty years. From that point on, they will present so many problems of maintenance that it will be necessary to pull them down and replace them."

The architectural cultures Korean architects explored have taught them how to combine an exploration of the most advanced syntax of modern architecture with an understanding and respect for established urban cultures. Many of them were able to adapt these lessons in the very different context of Korea, while also opening the way for foreign architects to learn about and contribute to the Korean urban fabric.

[1] Diana Cooper-Richet, Jean-Yves Mollier and Ahmed Silem, Passeurs culturels dans le monde des médias et de l'édition (XIXe s. et XXe s.), Villeurbanne, Presses de l'Enssib, 2005.
[2] Paul Carmignani (ed.), Figures du passeur, Perpignan, Presses universitaires de Perpignan, 2002.
[3] Caroline Maniaque Benton, interview with Kim Young-Joon, December 2013, Seoul.
[4] Some interviews used for this text were conducted by Caroline Maniaque and Tim Benton for the preparation of the exhibition, "Point-Contrepoint : Trajectory of Ten Korean Architects" (February-March 2014, Espace Callot/Ecole nationale supérieure d'architecture Paris-Malaquais) and for the book Caroline Maniaque Benton and Inha Jung (eds.), Point-Contrepoint : Trajectories of 10 Korean architects, Copenhagen, The Architectural Publisher B, 2014. Other interviews were conducted by Pier Alessio Rizzardi, for the exhibition and the book, The Condition of Seoul Architecture, Seoul, 2019.
[5] Caroline Maniaque and Tim Benton, Interview with Eun-Seok Lee, December 7, 2013, Seoul.
[6] Jacques Lucan, France, Architecture 1965-1988, Electa/Le Moniteur, 1989. The book was translated by Ji-Houng Han, Spacetime, Seoul, 2001. Han was a student of Jacques Lucan.
[7] Caroline Maniaque and Tim Benton, Interview with Sonjin Lee, December 10, 2013.
[8] Valérie Gelézeau, Séoul. Ville géante, cités radieuses, Paris, CNRS éditions, 2003, p. 12.
[9] Caroline Maniaque and Tim Benton, Interview with Ung-Won Yoon, December 5, 2013, Seoul.
[10] The website of Florian Beigel lists the Korea collaboration. http://aru.londonmet.ac.uk/
[11] See the exhibition "Citylandscapes". Architecture Foundation, Gallery of Modern Architecture, Economist Building, London, Sept. 22 – Oct. 7, 1995.
[12] Caroline Maniaque Benton, Interview with Jong-Kyu Kim, December 6, 2013, Seoul.
[13] Pier Alessio Rizzardi, Interview with Wook Choi, July 2017, Seoul.
[14] Pier Alessio Rizzardi, Interview with Wook Choi, July 2017, Seoul.
[15] Caroline Maniaque Benton, Interview with Wook Choi, December 5, 2013, Seoul.
[16] See Kenneth Frampton, Towards a Critical Regionalism: Six Points for an Architecture of Resistance, in Hal Foster (ed.), The Anti-Aesthetic. Essays on Postmodern Culture, Bay Press, Port Townsen, 1983.
[17] Pier Alessio Rizzardi, Interview with Jean Son, July 2017, Seoul.
[18] Caroline Maniaque and Tim Benton, Interview with Jean Son, December 2013, Seoul.
[19] Caroline Maniaque and Tim Benton, Interview with Jean Son, op.cit.
[20] Francesco Venezia, in ANAГKH Cultura e Storia delle Tecniche di Conservazione, n° 8, December 1994.

The Anti-Pop Typology

by Rafael Luna

Right page
Dongdaemun Design Plaza
Photo by Rafael Luna

Next page
Seoul represents the rapid growth of a city following western models for architecture novelty, only to produce the samw generic fabric.
Photo by Rafael Luna

The post-war era in the United States brought a sense of prosperity in economics and politics that founded the grounds for a consumerist society of conformity that was exemplified with the development of mass-produced suburbia, Levittown representing the quintessential prototype in this context. Intensified by the replacement of the radio for a television set in every living room, mass media, became the tool for the adoption of tv-dinners, Wonder Bread, and water-downed beer, products of mass-production over unique crafts. At the same time, a parallel world existed outside of this hygienic homogeneous mass-produced setting for which mass media became the vessel for spreading Rock and Roll, countercultures of unrest, civil rights movements, and political protests. Between these two clashes of worlds is where Pop-Art emerges as a social criticism of the time. By incorporating the imagery of the everyday items and consumer goods, Pop-Art would criticize society by means of appropriation. The incorporation of the ready-made and mass-produced elements into their art pieces allowed for mass appeal intent, that propagated within the popular culture.

Post-war architecture emerged from this same context as pop-art. The domino house became a replicable system of development that allowed for the adoption of mass-produced construction à la Ford. Through its rapid growth with newer construction techniques, the system became a style, shifting from Modernism to the International Style. This represented a popularization of the language of architecture into a mass appeal that spread through all scales and disciplines: modern city, modern skyscraper, modern furniture, and modern product design. Unlike pop-art, which represented a societal critique, Modernism became Pop, as in the popular style, and the popular understanding of space, not its critique. Its critique came from the counter projects of Postmodernism, Deconstructivism, and all the other styles and "ism's" that have been trying to move beyond the inescapable grasp of pop-architecture, which Modernism represents. Pop-architecture, in that sense, is more relatable to pop music today, which has been able to produce the majority of its top hits with the same four-chord progression - 1, 4, 5, 6 [1]. Modernism became a product of mass appeal, and adoption, comparable to pop-music, its language didn't change, the same grammar was used to compose variations, much like the top 100 pop hits. The underlying syntax did not come from the production of an original model. This presents a problem in contemporary practice as Modernism has become so ingrained in the architecture subconscious that 'contemporary' and 'modern' have been used interchangeably although they represent different languages. This has sparked the need to rediscover the dialogue in typology

within architecture.

The ambiguity between Pop architecture as popular architecture, or Pop architecture as one that pops in the urban context as a means of critique can only be evaluated by understanding the language of architecture through typology. There is a reason why architecture has become a repetitive exercise of outdoing previous models through the act of novelty in effects, but the lack of typological discussion impedes these buildings to really break away from just doing another Pop tune. To really be novel would require to explore the Anti-Pop typology. First, there must be an understanding of typology in itself, as there is the common misconception of use of typology as a classification of program and use. Building typology cannot be understood as a problem of the program, which Rossi described as a naive functionalism approach in 'The Architecture of the City' in 1966[2]. Yet, over half a century later, the program is frequently misused as a synonym to typology in architecture. Buildings can change programs over time, leaving the shell as the only remaining artifact, which can only be dissected through its elements, system, and form. These three categories make up the basis for language in architecture that can differentiate between architects falling under a Pop-trap or emerging as an Anti-Pop. Elements were introduced in the 18th century by two contemporaries, Abbe Laugier, and Jean-Nicolas-Louis Durand. Abbe Laugier discussed the relationship between man and nature and the need for man to protect himself from nature established the basis for any structure or architectural logic that could be composed of basic elements consisting of column, entablature, pediment, floors, windows, and doors. Jean-Nicolas-Louis Durand introduced an abstraction of architectural elements through his 'Précis des Leçons d'Architecture Données à l'École Royale Polytechnique'. As explained by Pier Vittorio Aureli[3], while at the Polytechnique, Durand was presented with the challenge of teaching architecture to engineering students employing a condensed seminar class. To do so, he cataloged architectural elements by types, including Laugier's idea of elements along with floor plans. This reduced architecture to taxonomy with the possibility of variation attributed to only the selection of different elements. The idea of elements has been ingrained into the subconscious of academia and practice, only varying by style. A wake-up call was presented during the 2014 Venice Biennale, curated by Rem Koolhaas, under the theme of 'Fundamentals', which shed light at the contemporary practice focusing on a variation of these same elements. It was also no coincidence that in the same Biennale just outside of the main exhibition entitled, 'Elements', a reproduction of the Maison

Domino was rebuilt as a wood structure. This is no coincidence because the Maison Domino represents the second component, systems in architecture. A system has to do with the way that space is constructed, meaning varying methods of fabrication and construction produce different spaces. As previously explained, the rapid adoption of the Maison Domino diagram as a system for rebuilding a post-war Europe, became a standard of systematic building. The Domino system presented a singular type of space, though, that could only vary with interior partitions or changing the facade. Yet, the language of the domino system remains the same no matter what facade is implemented regardless of the period. Here lies one of the main problems in contemporary practice, Pop-architecture is unable to recognize Modernism from Contemporanism. Practitioners driven by the allure of new methods of fabrication might install a digitally fabricated facade onto a modernist skeleton, in the naive hope that this facade effect will produce a contemporary building, but it is just slang within the modernist grammar. The system remains modernist; therefore, space remains modernist regardless of the facade intent. To compare to Pop-music, it is Max Martin, Swedish songwriter with the third most pop hits, writing a song for Taylor Swift or Katy Perry, and it makes no difference which artist performs it. The music notation might stay the same while changes happen in vocals, lyrics, or instrumentality. The underlying framework of chord progression does not change, guaranteeing a pop-hit. Although successful in music, in architecture, Pop becomes part of the generic urban fabric[4], part of the "garbage spill urbanism" as described by Patrik Schumacher[5], that can only be ordered utilizing the Anti-Pop. The Anti-Pop has been in development since post-modernism, as a series of critiques of the banal sterile environment that Modernism produced. As an analogous to Pop-Art and the ready-made assimilation, the New York Museum of Modern Art exhibited 'Architectural Fantasies' in 1967, where Hans Hollein presented montages of enlarged familiar objects onto landscapes as a direct critique to Modernism. This series of collage projects brought into perspective issues of form in architecture. The formal strategy being the last category for language in architecture. Modernism was more focused on the system than on form, therefore by enlarging an everyday object to the scale of the building, Hollein was immediately producing the sense of a new spatial logic that could not be conceived by the modernist system. This ready-made architecture mimics Pop Art, yet it remained stronger as visual art or critique, and not a realized building. If constructed, this formal approach would jump into the arena of Pop, as in kitsch. As a semiological problem, why would a building need to borrow a symbolic form to be a symbol in itself? The notorious debate between the "duck and the decorated shed" pinned by Brown, Venturi, and Izenour, a few years later in their 1972 canonical "Learning from Las Vegas" positioned a post-modernity feud in the language of architecture regarding this problem.[6]

Form in architecture, should not belong to neither the duck or the decorated. Both represent a kitsch sense of Pop and neither answers to a real dialogue with the urban fabric and spatial context[7]. Architecture does not need to adopt a literal graphical representation of an object to communicate, nor does it need to be a collage of graphical signs to be a symbol or signify. Form in architecture has intrinsic meaning to space, which was re-examined by Anthony Vidler in 1977 as "The Third Typology"[8]. Yet, the Modernism and the International Style spread like a virus in the reproduction of space, and not until the turn of the 20th century did form start to break from Modernism with a series of Dutch experiments on "Bigness", as described by Kees Christiaanse. The series of big projects that had sparked in Rotterdam during the 90's lead to an exploration of massing as a formal strategy between public and private space. Even though technology has improved in the development of elements, construction systems, that have allowed formal explorations concerning public and private space, the construction industry is still in a Fordist mode of mass production as a response to an ever-increasing urbanity, and the domino diagram still prevails as the popular starting point. Countries like Japan and Korea, which thrive in the Pop culture adoption, can replace their building stock every thirty years, allowing for newer buildings to implement new systems of construction that might allow novelty in spatial quality. Korea, for example, has been able to develop enough of the urban fabric to house twenty million people, yet the variation in design in newer buildings is found mainly through their

facades, while an inner modernist logic prevails[9]. Zaha Hadid Architects' Dongdaemun Design Plaza stands out among a sea of highrise buildings filled with commercial signs in a regenerated district of Seoul[10]. Already polemic, even before its conception, this behemoth of a building covers an entire city block where two stadiums once sat. Its fluid form deflects any traditional sense of elements such as windows, doors, roof, walls, or any clear reading of columns and slab system that fills all the neighboring buildings. The exuberant uniqueness of this building is often misunderstood as Pop in the sense of a shocking building concerning its context, like a pop-star. Instead, is an emblematic Anti-Pop typology that breaks from the popular, or kitsch understanding of architecture and urban space brought by trends, fads, and Modernism. The merger between elements, system, and form into a singular logic expresses a contemporary language of fluid space[11]. The notion of Contemporanism spreads from this logic of not repeating a Pop - popular - language, instead, creating its own. Buildings like Torre Agbar in Barcelona by Jean Nouvel, Taichung Opera House by Toyo Ito, Seattle Public Library by OMA, are all anti-pop typologies in the same fashion. In their explorations of escaping the traditional modern sense of space, these buildings have become icons in their respective cities. Their recognition has come from their separation and distancing from the generic Pop milieu. Pop has a recognizable flashiness that is easy to assimilate due to its repetitive language and ready-made adaptations. The Anti-Pop explores holistic spatial logic where form gets composed by a merger of elements and systems. Elements become openings, voids, in three-dimensional structural patterns that form spatial systems that can be parametrically adapted to their context and programs. This would relate more to an understanding of typology as a rule base logic that cannot be copied or repeated. These anti-pop typologies are unique and stand out from the generic not as novelties of affect, but as true transcenders to a new approach in architecture.

Right page
Gangnam Contrasts
Photo by the author

[1] https://youtu.be/nuGt-ZG39cU
[2] Rossi's development of urban theories lead to the establishment of Urban artifacts as the fundamentals for the reading of the city. This established a relationship between architecture form and city form.
[3] During his November 20, 2013 lecture at the AA, Pier Vittorio Aureli explained the standardization of Design under Durand's Precis. https://www.aaschool.ac.uk//VIDEO/lecture.php?ID=2227
[4] Seoul represents the rapid growth of a city following western models for architecture novelty, only to produce the same generic fabric. Photo by Rafael Luna.
[5] From Patrick Schumacher's lecture "Parametric Order—21st Century Architectural Order"
at Harvard GSD. https://youtu.be/zG2WMVkD5dw
[6] Analysis on Las Vegas as the basis for fomenting Postmodern theories.
[7] Handbag building in Sinsa, Seoul. Photo by Rafael Luna.
[8] Anthony Vidler's essay in Oppositions Reader 1998.
[9] Various highrise new developments around Seoul (D-Block, Sinsa Highrise, Hongik University). The international style prevails as a column and slab system, only to be covered by varying facade patterns and materials. Photos by Rafael Luna
[10] Dongdaemun Design Plaza by Zaha Hadid in the context of Dongdaemun. Photo by Rafael Luna.
[11] Dongdaemun Design Plaza. Photo by Rafael Luna.

Bibliography:
- Beato, Rick. "The Four Chords That Killed POP Music!" YouTube, 14 Dec. 2017, youtu.be/nuGt-ZG39cU.
- Rossi, Aldo. The Architecture of the City. MIT Press, 2007.
-Aureli, Pier Vittorio. "Architectural Association School of Architecture." AA Lectures Online, 9 Oct. 2015, www.aaschool.ac.uk//VIDEO/lecture.php?ID=2227.
- Schumacher, Patrik. "Patrik Schumacher, 'Parametric Order-21st Century Architectural Order.'" YouTube, 15 Feb. 2012, youtu.be/zG2WMVkD5dw.
- Venturi, Robert, et al. Learning from Las Vegas. The MIT Press, 2017.
- Vidler, Anthony. The Third Typology in Oppositions Reader: Selected Readings from a Journal for Ideas and Criticism in Architecture 1973-1984. Ed. Hays, K. Michael. Princeton Architectural Press, 1998.

In Conversation with Architects

Moon Hoon - *Moon Hoon Architects*
Gyoo Jang-yoon - *UnSangDong*
Kim Dong-jin & Kim Yoo-jung - *L'EAU design Co Ltd*

Cho Min-suk - *Mass Studies*
Kim Young-joon - *YO2 Architects*
Hwang Doo-jin - *Doojin Hwang Architects*

Kim In-cheurl - *Archium*
Cho Byoung-soo - *BCHO Architects*
Kim Min-ji - *ISON Architects*

Kim Hyo-man - *Iroje KHM Architects*
Kim Jun-sung - *Architecture Studio hANd*
Choi Moon-gyu - *GaA Architects*

Choi Wook - *ONE O ONE Architects*
Kim Jong-kyu - *M.A.R.U. network*
Ken Sungjin-min - *SKM Architects*

Kim Chan-joong - *THE_SYSTEM LAB*
Kim Seung-hoy - *KYWC Architects*
Lee Jeong-hoon - *JOHO Architecture*

Dogma vs Resiliency:
Architecture Beyond the Function

Contemporary architecture becomes an instantaneous image captured by a beautiful picture of an internationally recognized photographer. It is obvious to say that this image does not correspond to the reality of real physical architecture, or how it is used or evolves.

From a very technical environment of the past, architects opened up to the logic of creative foreign universities, getting into contact with new theories and discovering new possibilities. Once back, they had to deal with the problems of the local urban landscape, which requires moving away from both academia and professional technical attitude.

They observe the built environment, the speed of change, and the evolution of culture, starting to criticize the functional dogmatic concepts that no longer correspond to the current situation. Society is fast and consumerist, and architects must adapt and respond to the dynamism of relationships and constant changes in the use of architecture.

With the technology that influences contemporary society, space changes from physical to intangible and set on communication-based relationships, constantly changing the architectural program. Architects must rethink the *raison d'être* of the function, revolutionizing the composition and layout of the building, while avoiding creating an immediately obsolete space. Passing through the evolution of the meaning of function, starting from "form follows function" to the Mies' "Universal Space", Khan's revolution of "Served Spaces" and arriving at today with Koolhaas' the "Internal Conceptual Duality" mediated by buffer zones, architects try to add to it and find the new way.

The most advanced experiments conducted by the architects explore how to deal with function in contemporary architecture without falling into previous failures. They try to shift the attention from functionality to spatial quality, looking for a multiplicity of spatial narratives, in which the function is not fixed in advance, but spaces become supports of new social dynamics, creating places and stimulating new functions.

They draw from resilient references in which the structure remains the same, but space can be used in diversified ways; the winning places of urban environments are areas that remain strongly unchanged while the function changes over time. To create these narratives, they refer to the logic of the media, interdisciplinarity, artistic and surreal references, rules of cinematographic, and photographic composition; both referring to contemporary art and deeply rooted traditional art and architecture, which determine new compositional interpretations and a reflection on points of view and perspectives. They explore the sensation of architectural elements and the material concept, considering the sensations perceived by people, the overlapping systems and spatial logic unrelated to a function, aiming at creating a narrative capable of self-generating situations.

The experience comes from great surprise that finds the balance between different forces.

When I give a presentation, I often get surprising reactions from people. They laugh a lot! People had thought architecture was a serious matter, but after I explained it in a simple, understandable and fun way, they have a new understanding, and suddenly they start to see architecture as a more accessible subject.

Moon Hoon
Moon Hoon Architects

Enjoying Design with Humor
Fresher Look at Architecture
Eternal Inconsistency
Inspirations Are Everywhere
Doodle My Way to The Moon

Moon Hoon Interview
Photo by the author

Enjoying Design with Humor

[...] I think I became a kind of humorist architect. When I give a presentation, I often get surprising reactions from people. They laugh a lot! I believe the primary observation - from seeing people who are coming to my exhibition or visit my buildings - is that they enjoy my presentations because they are really funny to start with. I have the feeling that people in general usually had thought architecture was a serious matter, but somehow after I explain it in a straightforward, understandable and funny way, they seem to have a new understanding and suddenly start to see architecture as a more approachable subject. I'm sure that ordinary people who don't have a specific design background or those who are not professional architects, can enjoy design very directly and at a new level, with humor and light up things.

Fresher Look at Architecture

How is the architectural narrative affecting the people?

For instance, when I describe my architecture, I don't start as a boring description of functions, quantities, and dimensions, because I think it is not effective. For instance, in one of my projects, the musician of an amateur rock group [Rock It Suda] commissioned me a cluster of buildings. I took the challenge, and I developed it according to different themes [Spain, Barbie, stealth, Ferrari, cave, and traditional Korean house]. In [the Spanish] one there are two big horns at each side, and when I presented this project, I start saying, "It's a horny house... ooh!". Horny house, [Laughs] and the people get it. It arrives directly at them and also they can interpret it in other different ways. So people that I meet, other fellow architects, or even somebody outside the architecture world, they get these inspirations from me. I don't know whether as an architect or a lecturer or presenter, but I saw that I'm able to inspire people to go beyond conventional architecture and to reach another dimension of understanding. By using architecture, I'm able to send out messages on what I understand about the world through architecture. I hope that sometimes people would be inspired by it... and what they hear and see could be an inspiration for a fresher look at architecture. Not only that, but I want them to have a new way of seeing that goes beyond architecture itself. It is useful to see things beyond the constrictions of society and academia to have expended convey of ideas. This can relate only to architecture and design, but it can also be in many different aspects of our life.

Which kind of reaction do you observe in people?

Sometimes during presentations, I get questions so diverse from the audience. Some people ask why you use this red color, why do you use a horn or what is the meaning of a specific shape... They ask me philosophical questions too. All this energy is inspiring for everybody. So I imagine that in my work, I might be able to convey and to give an inspirational message, not just about canonic architecture, but sometimes through many different layers and unpredicted aspects.

Eternal Inconsistency

How would you define the context here in Seoul?

To understand the context in Seoul, you need to see it as energy. I often talk

Rock It Suda
Photo by Kim Yong-kwan

about Seoul as a liquid entity, meaning... it is not actually liquid, but if you take a timespan and run it very quickly, you see that the next building is going away in 2 or 3 years. So your neighborhood is disappearing, and new buildings are coming in. If you consider those contexts that you see as stable or durable, you are wrong, because soon they will be gone forever. The system in which we live and work is always in a fluctuating situation. What follows is that, as expected when you design a building, you can reference to not so many things. So what do you want to do? You can embrace this situation and go deeper in your inner thoughts or towards your inner being, and this is much greater than your context nearby. Out of this situation, you can see why drastically new architecture can be born, because most of the time we are in a place where immediate context doesn't really have any relevance. This dynamism that you can reference from means there is a flux of ideas coming from many energies and somehow crashing and clashing. So, when you design, you need to be internal... you need to be like a monk! [Laughs] Or you have to reach out far, and far away from your culture to bring some exotic ideas and mix it in here.

Joint to a fluctuating context, Seoul has one of the strictest legislation. How do you deal with it?

I act according to the rules, but I play around them... For example, the regulation is based on the construction limits derived from the road views. There are construction limits that form diagonals starting from the roads around and other diagonals coming from other buildings. They create a more or less complicated pyramid shape; so we know where the limit is. Basically, if you build a maximum volume, the resulting form will come from it... First of all, I'm not saying: "I want to fight against this rule!". Even if it is a strange shape and it is difficult or yet absurd to comply with. What I do is that I just accept it. I play with the volumes inside the boundaries at first and then if I want to go outside, and yoo-hoo! I do movable architecture. I go out and come back with building parts, and I move up and down - because the regulation doesn't precisely pronounce about moving parts. For instance, if the people come around and say your building is beyond the limit, I move the parts outside, and I hide. Whatever the rules are, you can always play around it... It is not to make the statement that I'm cynical about it. But I'm saying: "why not?".

Inspirations Are Everywhere

How do you start a project?

I start in the city, with the regulation. I make with SketchUp 3d boundaries in a red transparent box, so we know where the limit is. To develop the design, I try to get inspired by a variety of different things. But sometimes I get also inspired from the client. I observe the situation, the appearance, their look, and if they are a couple or a group, I observe their dynamics. For example, if the wife of the client has a big hat, and I find it interesting, I ask myself, "Might it have something to do with the site?" Or if the husband and wife have some troubles with their relationship, I envision the house with two "heads", a kind of "Never Meeting House". These two parts avoid and negate each other, and when the composition comes together, they become friends again. I try to get inspiration from whatever thing I can.

Which are the effects of these unconventional spaces on people?

Rock It Suda
Photos by Hoon Yeum-seung

There are a lot of playful elements I put in the design. For example, picture a diagonal like the shoulder bag I'm wearing now. Diagonal means movement, right? In the house, diagonal mains connection, like a staircase. In my designs, I use a lot of active platforms and levels in many ways. These naturally make movement easy, creating a lot of dynamism and interpreting the usage of the building. I also work with scale and dimension. I include several double or triple height spaces, several light volumes or elements that are occupying these vertical space all the way. You can call these spaces atrium for events or the basic structure of the architecture... it can be even something small. When I design, I try to envision a lot of visual channels in the space because it gives the depth to the perception of the architecture... I try to bring dizziness! Because I like kind of space that is really 3-D and for me, 3-D really means a design that can give you vertigo, a space where you feel that you might fall... and you might fly back up! [Laughs]. If there is a space that doesn't give you this kind of felling, that is only a 2d space. For me, this is the 3-D space: an extreme space of experience. I believe that is because we are more sensitive to height than width. A lot of my architecture, I think, has the attitude towards an unbalanced approach, to create a vertical, or diagonal experience or even a spiral experience. [...]

Are you inspired by some traditional aspect of Korean architecture?

I take a lot of inspirations from traditional architecture, especially from the logic in itself. The first essential characteristic which I observed is how high-tech this ancient architecture really is. It has openness and closeness, they have the technology that can open up shutters and walls all the way to create a maximum penetration... they can even fold up! I learned from their lightness and the sense of scale, the small courtyards inside the house, and several different types of small-scale variations. As well as the ups and downs of the ground has the little movements of structure and pavement. Because, if you look at the internal structure of ancient houses, there is a lot of action involved. Even with the doors, we need to move up and down to cross the doorstep, and you have to push yourself, ritually before entering or exiting. Sometimes when you come through the door, you have to bend your neck. So I think these are ideas I've always taken into consideration in my designs. Also, the overall shape within itself doesn't actually mimic the whole shape of the house, such curvature. I like these kinds of floating ideas, how the house is on stilts and the entire structure looks like it's floating. This is the model of home I'm building now [Butterfly House/Crab House]. If we look at the model, we can see how it best represents what I was describing - the composition of the space, and even representing well the shape. I designed this house for a retired professor and his wife. It was supposed to be a kind of inspiration from a butterfly floating and flapping its wings, but it looks like a crab instead! [Laughs]. What I want to show you is that even if the shape is a bit unconventional, the form recalls vernacular attached roof house. Here the unique qualities of the traditional idea of the house are implemented with: a courtyard with a specific scale, and there is a pavilion above the roof. It is acting as a thumb up pushed out... A floating pavilion, pushing forward to the future! So all these quality concepts are included here in this compact form... I'm talking about these references from the past because traditional architecture has influenced my experience to visit old traditional architecture and it has inspired some aspects of my design composition... But usually, to be honest, I don't explicitly explain this, and I don't say that is the representation of Korean identity or any other thing... no, no-no! I'm not consciously going to say, "I'm going to be the translator of traditional architecture!" I'm describing these concepts and how I integrated them in my design may be only afterwards.

Simple House
Photos by Sun Nam-goong

Simple House
Photo by Sun Nam-goong

Doodle My Way to The Moon

Which were the experiences that over the years particularly shaped your way of designing?

There were several significant revelations for me. One was when I was really young, and one day, I realized that I could draw perspectives in 3-D. Wow, nobody had taught me! I can push the point of view, and it was much more real. In primary school, I was looking at children newspapers, and there was competition saying to use the letter "M" to draw something. I draw down cars and busses shaped as "M", and I won. I was always winning first prizes, and after the third time, they said: "please do not send any more drawings because you're winning every time" [Laughs]. So I realize I was able to manipulate everything in every other object, seeing something simple and transforming it into something else... Another time I was in high school in Hobart [Australia]. I was sketching every day, and I was a bit lonely, I guess. As a teenager, I would spend my weekends drawing watercolors, like 30 paintings in the summer... I brought back the sketches to my teacher, Peter Bronston - a British professor - and he said: "You did so many drawings. I like your work. We have to do an exhibition!". I never thought before that I could do an exhibition. As a student, you don't believe it's possible, but he said: "I'll help you to have an exhibition, Mr. Moon". I had an exhibition in my school library, and it was a big surprise because the people were buying the paintings. My exhibition was almost sold-out. So I became a professional artist at the age of 16, and I got commissions too. I had commissions to draw paintings from my friend's parents. They called me and said, "you are the kid!"

How essential are the drawings for your architecture?

I think drawings has a meaning in itself. If I have to describe them, I need to categorize them. For example, I'm not doing architectural drawings for a commission but for architecture itself... like the walking pavilions. It's a drawing that could be built in the future that could envision something or it can be an end product by itself. I can imagine how it performs, or moves, and I found it extremely useful to be able to visualize this space. Other types are usually done when I draw inspirations by what I've built already. Meaning I created a building, and after the competition, I'm inspired by it. I could have done it in many different ways, and I start to imagine other possibilities. So these potentials are translated into drawings, and they can be re-translated in a possible future built project. The third type of drawings might be something very trivial. I am always carrying my "doodle book". I draw up what catches my eyes, and I elaborate it, turning it into architecture. So for example when I was in Brussels I had a lot of mussel soup, it is very famous there, and you can see in my "doodle book" I drew a mussel architecture! [Laughs]. I like to explore my mind and see as many meanings as possible. It [mussel architecture] could have a sexual meaning, or the two shells locking can give you an idea of closed up, shyness or introversion. The food I had eaten can be translated into a real blown-out architecture or can be summarized in the kind of food architectural diagram!... When I was at RMIT University [in Melbourne], I had a really great time. When I had to develop my thesis, I was really contentious. I chose one of the bridges in Seoul - there were 11 bridges at the time - and I started noticing they were all orange and blue. I wanted to take a big can of paint and make it red. I tried to start from making it surreal; turning everyday objects into different things by using only paint. Then I introduced in the project a

Wind House
Photo by Sun Nam-goong

Wind House
Photo by Sun Nam-goong

Love Hotel, a nightclub on top and a crematorium. You could climb on top of the nightclub, and you would see the traffic jam; you see the cars with the red light, looking like a drawing that came out from Japanese animation. The cars start to look like bugs walking around, and suddenly you notice the flying bridge in front of you. You see this scenario, and suddenly, you feel you are drawn. Somebody say "jump!" and you jump. You fall down, having a kind of suicide experience. When you're dead, you're burnt in the crematorium, and you're absorbed as energy, and you're reincarnated... to run the Love Hotel. [...]

Lollipop House
Photos by Sun Nam-goong

Lollipop House
Photo by Sun Nam-goong

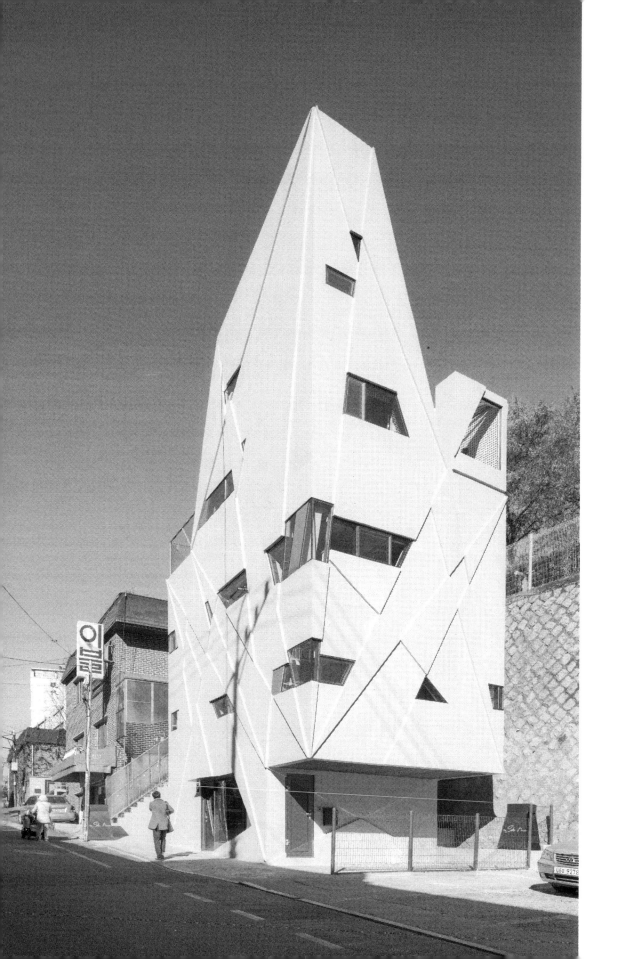

Left page
Dogok Maximum
Photo by Sun Nam-goong

Top right page
Queens Bucket
Drawing by Moon Hoon

Bottom right page
Dogok Maximum
Photo by Sun Nam-goong

Sang Sang Museum
Photo by Kim Yong-kwan

Sang Sang Museum
Photos by Kim Yong-kwan

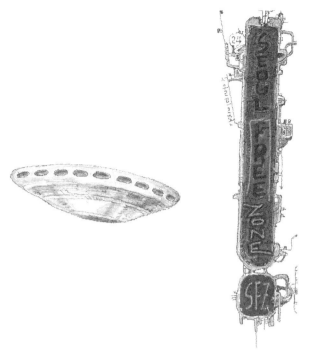

This page
Seoul Free Zone
Drawing by Moon Hoon

Next left page
102 Nabile Dream
Drawing by Moon Hoon

Next top right page
Mussels Space Ship House
Drawing by Moon Hoon

Next bottom right page
Mussels Space Ship House
Model
Courtesy of Moon Hoon

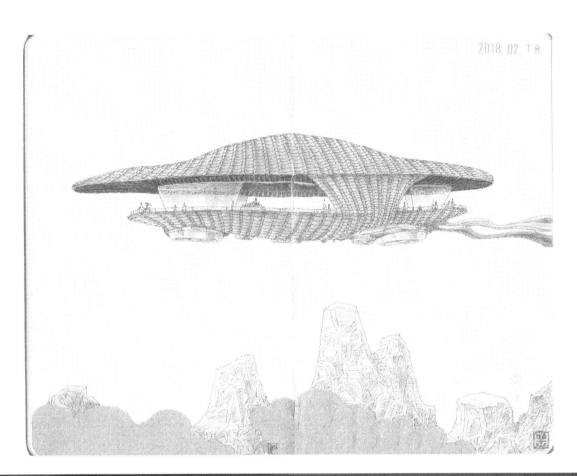

Left page
Body Shop

Right page
Ntsa Stone
Drawings by Moon Hoon

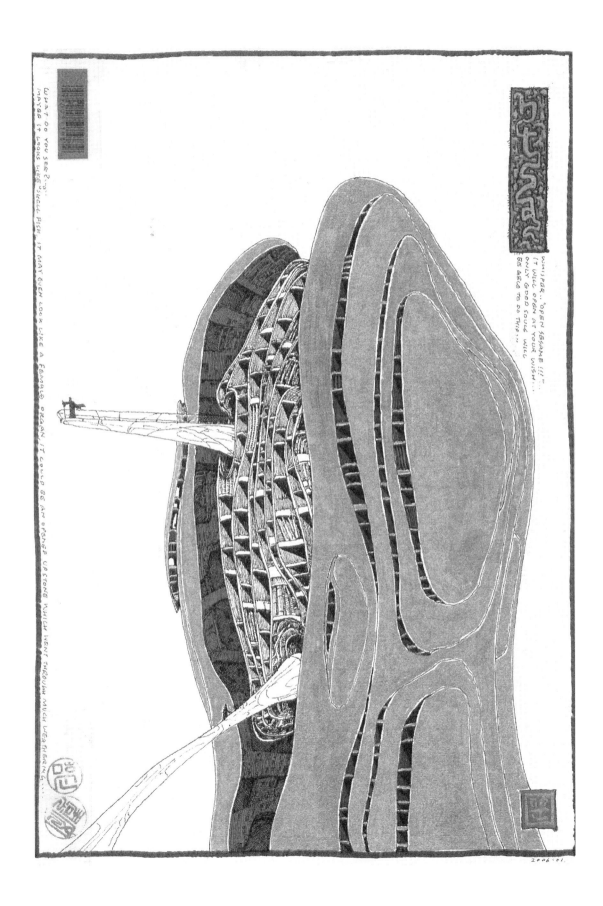

My intention is to introduce the "Deleuzian Fold" in the social and architectural realms. Here the fold is no longer a shape. The "Fold" is a quality, like a pleat-producing reciprocal structure, changing and offering random bends in the continuity of the flat space and opening up spatial possibilities considered impossible in the past.

Jang Yoon-gyoo
UnSangDong

Compound Body
Becoming an Animal
Self-Transforming
Skin Scape
Clip City

Jang Yoon-gyoo Interview
Photo by the author

Compound Body

In Seoul, we see a peculiar coexistence of multiple historical layers. We had come to a schizophrenic condition of the context in which we must conceive a new way of analyzing, to create new concepts to build architecture. We are in the exact moment when new transformations and explorations are necessary, and we need to take advantage of the infinite contemporary opportunities. It would be impossible to have a new perspective through conventional research practices. The entire field of architecture must be questioned and investigated, looking for an original analyzing method. At the beginning of 2000, I wrote some books on the new vision of the city, which became the starting point of my current architectural thinking.

In your writings, it often appears "Compound Body" as a fundamental concept in the creation of your architecture.

"Compound Body" is a type of architecture that integrates different points of view to open up possibilities and produce unexpected results. I start from examining a system considering it unstable and therefore, uncertain, which can generate a series of opportunities to create innovative effects... I believe architecture is a system that embraces potentially all the possibilities available. We must not limit our possibilities but expand them.

How is this process operating?

We must start by rewriting the foundations of the architectural space, starting with the understanding of the relationships between systems and logics of different urban territories and social landscapes. The world is constantly evolving, oscillating between a state of instability and stability, and architecture must face these issues. This new approach deals with organizations deriving from numerous sources, origins, and various fields. It is a system that transcends a priori connections and always tries to encourage new reinterpretations.

How to develop this system?

Currently, in the architectural scene, there is an effort to develop interdisciplinary relationships and to work in the blur between disciplines. I do the same... but I also try to create new personal and unique definitions. [...] There is a massive amount of information coming from the media, in some ways encyclopedic but at the same time random and seemingly endless. In this system, we have the prerequisites of creating a constant and evolutionary definition of logic, interpretations, and connections, continually seeking logic in this apparent chaos. I think that the architect should assume the role of mediator by mending the discrepancies between different boundaries of disciplines and concepts placed at the antipodes. [...] Traditional architectural practice had always been a tool of expressing a self-identity. But it does not have to be like that anymore... Through the online network, the world forms one single linkage, and it is becoming less acceptable to discuss single values and individual activities. Therefore, we must understand the value of the new current condition and this implies recognizing the world as a unique structure and a field of knowledge [...]. We must think about which materials and ingredients to begin with, before discussing mixed strategies [...]. We have to catch this new opportunity, rather than merely repeating "previous exercises" in superficial ways.

How to do it?

For me, the spirit of modernity is not so much based on formal rebellion, but rather the attempt to materialize aspects of integration of technology into space... The spirit of modernism consists of a framework of integration among structure, space, material, skin, landscape, etc. Now the rapid development of technology provides even brighter potential for us to approach this goal. It is not so difficult to imagine the world operated by technology, space, and property in one single continuous flow and, in architecture, such attempts are already being made through works all over the globe. [...] The result will be a space structured on experience or narrative. It could be structured on a continuous möbius-like space, eliminating the distinction between inside and outside. [...] I found it interesting that Escher's loop physically substitutes double-coded conceptions, transposing the fictional code of the world into architectural articulation. It is a space that reminds us of an idea of ceaselessly moving structure, an experience that reconnects to the city dynamics. A practical example is to generate different types of architecture using two different "program-concepts". If we start from social observation and the urban phenomenon, we can propose methods of interpretative selection and integrations of different elements. The result may not be a single space, but of convergent situations and combinations of the many. In this way, the architectural space becomes an infinitely continuous structure; an infinite sequence of voids that generate and organize the space... The will is to avoid distinctions and to create tendencies to integration. The second part of the constitution of "Compound Body" space results from the alchemy of these different "substances". [...] Personally, I achieve it through a kind of catalyst, or mixing the "substances", which - almost accidentally - creates a "reaction". The architectural quality acquired combines with the possible integration of today's available technology... Observing the genetic engineering nanotechnology, we recognize how these efforts generate new "outcomes" and transformations... So human beings are transformed and the "man" we've known so far, and he is no longer the one we think he is... We live in a society where all boundaries - like time and space - evolve, and humans evolve with them.

Becoming an Animal

How this contemporary "man" had become?

... An indistinct species. He is irritated and with a desire for a different world. How does man perceive and react to a social environment and relationships with the generated space? The point is that instead of reading only what the new space can generate - or terminate - we should analyze what causes this result and how to predict the possible future evolutions... My analysis must begin with a willingness to search for invisible codes, consisting of future experiments and theorizing what happens in our current status. Because I think it's fundamental to catch up with the modern by transcending the modern, and my idea of the man "Becoming Animal", is the result of this catching-up and transcending this new environment.

How to interpret these changes?

It is our duty to look for new compositions and approaches in architecture. These can derive from urban planning issues, architectural practice, or experimental research... all that can generate new spatial typologies. Evidently, this is a strategy that finds solutions, codes through a process. That is why I identify this as "Becoming Animal", and not as "To Be Animal" - "Becoming" indicates the system

This page
Concept Sketches
Drawings by Jang Yoon-gyoo

Next Page
**Hand's Performance for
Communication**
Photo by Jang Yoon-gyoo

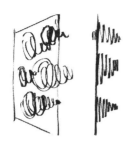

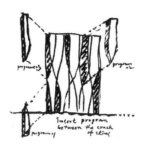
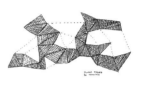

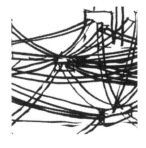

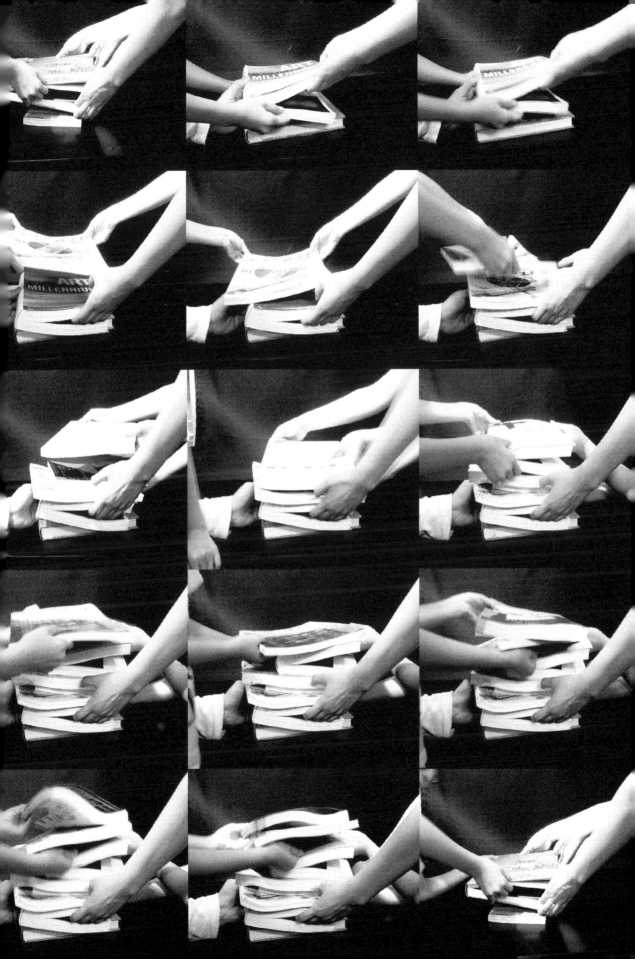

Life & Power Press
Photo by Sun Nam-goong

Life & Power Press
Photo by Sun Nam-goong

of possibilities to bring out new knowledge and creativity instead of creating a unique solution. At the same time, "Becoming" denies many aspects of Western philosophy such as eternity, universality, fundamentalism, and essentialism.

Self-Transforming

How does this translate into built space?

The intention is to introduce the "Deleuzian Fold" into social and architectural realms. Here the fold is no longer a form. The "Fold" is a quality, like a pleat-producing reciprocal structure, mutating and offering random bends into the continuity of flat space, and opening up spatial possibilities regarded as impossible in the past. [...] It looks like a space that completely separates itself from an idea of a program. In fact, "Programmatic Mutation" is one example. We already know that a bathroom can become a café, a house or an office - it is not a radical new concept anymore. Rather than any specific will of the architect, these hybridized space is the result of everyday life... These spaces become hybrids where functions quickly get reshuffled by social demands and circumstances. A more critical issue, however, is to take the given framework and explore where we can reach in terms of creating new spatial possibilities or urban articulations. [...] It is also along with the program's self-transforming capability rather than satisfying the demands of form or structure. [...] Space can organize and arrange its own sets of hybrid programs, or make attempts to create a manifold independency from a formal or programmatic relationship. Embracing these possibilities, we allow architectural models to transform and therefore to bring up a series of questions about its fundamental methodology of assembling programs into architectural spaces. [...]

Skin Scape

Your buildings do not blend with the surrounding context. How do you keep this in mind during the design?

"Form" is not my purpose... I believe there is a strong relationship between the facade and the context, especially from how people perceive the architecture and what effect architecture has on them. In reality, it is much more complicated than that. [...] A facade is a tool of interconnection between architecture and the city. Therefore, the quality of a facade affects the quality of a city. The composition of the facade can also influence both a specific building function or the public space next to the building. We are aware that architectural spaces are in a constant process of revision as a kind of "body without organs", but to go one step further, when we consider the space in the digital age, it could maximize even more the potential of the "skin". Different from the past, the facade has become a subject of discussion in today's architecture... We cannot let the facade be only a pattern or formal solution... We need to explore new strategies able to create a positive impact and revolutionize the structure of our cities.

How do you use the facade to create a pragmatic impact?

We should start to recognize the city as a continuity of architectural "skins" and let's observe it... There is a current trend of blurring between what is real and what is virtual, and the concept of facade could be reimagined, giving us possibilities to enter another dimension - where the skin materializes as a reaction between the limits of a "double-sided reality". The potential hidden in the facade is to become a code to declare a new type of space. Physical features in architecture such as

Gallery Yeh
Photo by Kim Yong-kwan

columns, walls, floors can be understood not as individual elements, but as part of a whole. In the same way, the facade may have no differentiation between the roofs, floors, and walls - or any other architectural element. If one is capable, this freedom can be expanded to infinity! Imagine for a moment to design a space like Escher's drawings. There are points of gravity that govern the space, but here they are contradicted... creating a non-gravitational space, a space generated by the acknowledged freedom in architectural composition... We could develop it further in continuous facades, continuous "skins" - which I call "non -gravitational skin" - a tool capable of removing any reference of space [...]. In my mind, the skin is a porous element and an ambiguous surface, characterizing the richness and underlining spatial qualities generated here... Walls, floors, and ceilings do not differ, but they are only continuous skins, becoming not only an architectural space, but also communication, creating an impact on the urban organization of the city.

Clip City

I am particularly interested in knowing step by step your inspirational process.

We need to break the a priori structures. I have always used the strategy of observing the city as a union of all events and phenomena.... I want to show you a book I've written called "Clip City"... This is a research tool using the urban environment as a source of inspiration. Here, I created a vocabulary of all the concepts and ideas refering to the urban situation... It can be described as a kind of library or a catalog of Asian and Western cities' characteristics - because this topic is already-chaotic-enough. My "Clip City" methodology is based on disassembling, and disintegrating the urban "text" into small pieces and relatively simplifying it. I composed a very long disassembly of the components from "A to Z" to produce thousands of "texts", describing specific urban characteristics. In this perspective, a city is no longer a city, but has become a structure of "texts" that singularly belongs beyond its meaning. Singularly taken, they become more agile and await a new reading and potential evolution.

You have tried to simplify the complexity of the city to find a new complex interpretation...

Yes, to find new possibilities. In practice, we can choose inside the list of specific items, and these can stimulate your imagination. Depending on the project, I can compare several essential characteristics, I can then combine them and conclude the features and phenomena.... A very erratic approach that leads us to see the city through a specific element, leaving behind all the others. For example, we can analyze the item "car", this word and its problematic connotation that could lead us to reconsider this topic from a completely different point of view, such as the driver's seat. We can also isolate the car-system mentally and observe how it develops in the city and how it interacts with other systems such as green spaces, buildings and so on.... Remove from your mind everything that is not related and imagine a city only made by streets... The results can be of powerful inspiration, both critically and proactively... For this process I was deeply inspired by Hans Ulrich Obrist, that described the city of Seoul in his writings as a "Moving Media" experience and a method of translating hidden urban codes through the use of different media.

Gallery Yeh
Photo by Kim Yong-kwan

This and next page
Study Models
Courtesy of UnSangDong

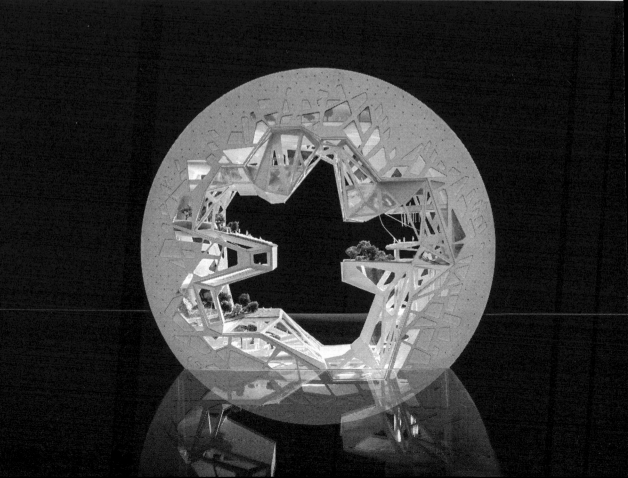

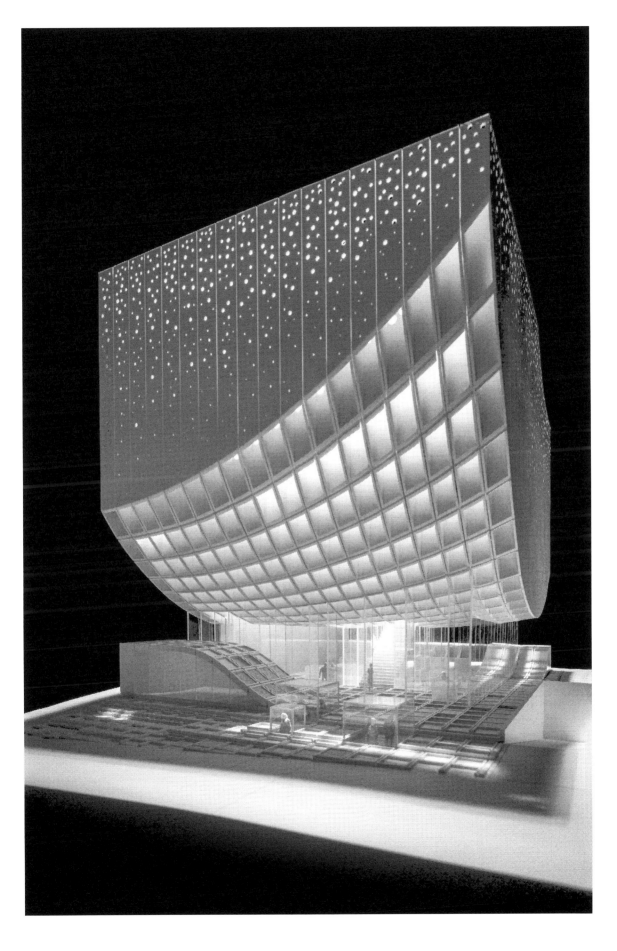

The goal is not to create "Universal Space" but "Multi-universal Spaces", in which logic and sub-logics could coexist, generating spaces with blurred boundaries and overlapping with other systems. If you look at Kandinsky's paintings, many different ideas create different overlying episodes, which could inspire new design systems.

Kim Dong-jin &
Kim Yoo-jung
L'EAU design

Multi-universal Space

Kim Dong-jin &
Kim Yoo-jung Interview
Photo by the author

Multi-universal Space

[...] A city can be described as a community full of different entities. But if architecture is strangled by economic logic, it becomes an icy object that can no longer respond to the variety of changes in the environment and to social stimuli...

How to design an architecture that meets this current condition?

In 2000, after studying in France, I opened my own studio. When the first project arrived, I listened to the client, talking about their wishes and the space they wanted me to design. [...] I immediately noticed a problem and gradually began to understand the need to distance myself from both the academic world and the way other colleagues usually design. I began to observe how the current practices insist too much on the function to create both composition and language. From the beginning, I always criticized Sullivan's model "the form follows the function". [...] With Mies van der Rohe, the architects began to exploit the potential of the open plan to create a "universal space" in which the function was not predetermined, creating an architectural environment where "anything can happen". With Luis Khan, the logic has reversed; people understood the possibility of an architectural layout subdivided into distinct spaces, but connected by a "service space" where "anything could happen"... At the beginning of my professional career, I had all these different ideas in my mind and other things... It was a difficult period for me culturally. To make sense of all the learned concepts and the requests of the clients, and that drives me into researching for more...

What conclusions did you draw from your research?

I realized that these views were not updated and that each one of them had profound weaknesses. Little by little with my work, I started to understand in depth the logic behind the space, and I made several attempts to design architectures that consider logics and current dynamics we observe in society. Today we have arrived at a particular situation in which architecture can potentially already reach far beyond these concepts. If we continue to design like in the past, space will suffer in terms of quality and vitality, becoming undefined and sloppy.

How to design for the present and the future?

We need to understand the role of an architect to be someone who designs "living" spaces able to communicate with people. We must keep in mind the lessons of the past and try to introduce new narratives of space, to characterize the environment and increase the possibility of connection between different spaces. [...] It's a bit like when a novelist develops a plot. But, in this situation, in addition to the main plot, the reader can make different interpretations by reading different storylines. In the same way, the architect can give a particular narrative to the building, and the inhabitant could experience it in completely different ways through the freedom of personal interpretation. In the most successful projects of mine, I observe people, finding new definitions of the spaces I designed. The more this happens, the more I feel fulfilled and having achieved my goal... Unlike Mies, my aim is not to create "universal space" but "multi-universal spaces", where logic and sublogics could coexist, generating spaces with blurred boundaries and overlapping with other systems. If you look at Kandinsky's paintings, many different ideas

create different overlying episodes, imagining new systems of designs. It is also similar when a film is developed or in a television series... In a movie, there is usually a well-defined plot, where little can be interpreted and imagined. Instead, "Multi-Universal Spaces" is much more similar to the television series in which the characters are the real center of attention, and it is possible to develop stories in continuous evolution. If we superimpose different "architectural characters", we can generate narratives and, if they are strong enough, they could have the role of a program generator, keeping up with the constant evolutions and breaking any possible limitation.

I was particularly interested in talking about the Nonhyun Matryoshka project and its continuity and spatial potential.

Exactly... here is an influential spatial narrative. The proximity of the surrounding influenced the result of the building. To avoid any violation of privacy, we averted any direct visual connection. The project consists of vertical concrete "ribbons" that allow only vertical permeability, with the skylight and natural elements. All the spaces are made up of many different programs in which each space has its well-defined character - not function. Just like the Russian doll Matrioska, the project consists of a box-in-a-box structure and a story-in-story composition. Spaces are structured in parallel with infinite correlations, bringing, at the same time, external and internal characters.

How could you generate these generic functions but with well-defined features?

The client didn't assign any specific program to the building. Spaces are available for people to use for commercial activities... Usually, the best conditions are always on the ground floor or at most on the first level above ground. We have studied a system of connections and ramps, creating an excellent continuous connection with the public realm. At the same time, the joints are made from open spaces such as gardens and terraces, that replicate the conditions of the ground floor. Inside we wanted to give a feeling of twisted spatial continuity, so the stairs are taking different directions, space opens and closes, becoming external and internal, commercial and public.

Why is it so important to create complexity in the space?

By creating an unpredictable "multi-universe" space, people can explore the building and are very unlikely to encounter repetitive areas. People will be in a constant state of discovery, increasing their excitement and willingness to explore more the architecture.

Previous, this and next page
Nohyun Matryoshika
Photo by Kim Yong-kwan

Next pages
Tropism of Wild Flower
Photo by Park Wan-soon

Jeju Bayhill Pool & Villa
Photo by Sun Nam-goong

Jeju Bayhill Pool & Villa
Photo by Sun Nam-goong

Jeju Bayhill Pool & Villa
Photo by Sun Nam-goong

There is a polarization of two camps: the "Systematic", huge companies responsible for 99% of the built environment and the "heterogeneous", smaller studies interested in a certain type of discourse. The first group is brave, but they feel guilty because they don't have enough time. The latter are very sensitive, but also angry because they cannot create a certain impact.

Cho Min-suk
Mass Studies

Crow's Eye View: the Korean Peninsula
Multiplicity Between Art, Architecture and Society
Systemic vs Heterogeneous
The Double Gaze

Cho Min-suk Interview
Photo by the author

Crow's Eye View: the Korean Peninsula

The national pavilions at the Biennale that year were given the agenda of "Absorbing Modernity: 1914-2014." One hundred years ago, Korea was a single nation under the colony of Japan. So it seemed to us that focusing only on the South would have been neglecting half of the story. By including North Korea in the exhibition, we were able to work with a multitude of architects, artists, scholars, and cultural liaisons to contribute prints, photographs, and rich stories. To be more explicit about works by North Koreans, we were able to have prints and paintings, and also commissioned works - a comic book, collected and coordinated by one of our participants, Nick Bonner, Director of Koryo Tours, Beijing.

How did such a collaboration take place?

Nick was able to orchestrate the comic book by commissioning a North Korean artist, who consulted with local architects to come up with a story, titled "A Day of an Architect." The outcome was a short booklet, without text or description. The story begins with an architect presenting an important project called "Future 1," to which he receives an enthusiastic standing ovation and is awarded the commission. There is another character in the story, a very young girl who admires the architect and wants to follow in his footsteps. She works very hard, day and night, and dreams of also designing an important building. What follows is the description of the agony in creating her work. Suddenly, she sees a maple leaf and has a Eureka moment, shaping the concept for her project. At the end of her hard work, she presents a high-rise building called "Hope 1," and is also rewarded. It's a simple story. In the North, these kinds of comics are made for children, to instill ideology. Kim Jong-Il, the father of Kim Jong-Un, the current North Korean leader, had created a kind of renaissance for the arts, architecture, music, and cinema. He composed a manifesto on architecture, stating that architecture could and should resemble nature - which is clearly an important part of the narrative in this comic book.

The exhibition received the Golden Lion for Best National Participation that year.

I think the work at the Biennale was a kind of miracle and we all hoped for a step towards the beginning of a possible dialogue and cultural exchange between the North and South through architecture. I don't know how much you know about Korean history, but earlier this year was the impeachment of former President Park. It was at the very beginning of her government that I had been appointed as commissioner of the Korean Pavilion and began to curate the exhibition. It seemed to us that this was the right moment to involve the North, as they were a couple of years into a new leadership with Kim Jong-Un, and the South had appointed a new president with President Park, who had just started a mandate on 'trust-building' towards peace. Still, I remained sensitive and tried to play it down, simply presenting it as 'an architecture exhibition, nothing more.' We had to report and clear research materials and exhibition content, basically everything, with the Ministry of Unification, and as you can imagine, it was a very sensitive situation throughout. The fact that the exhibition was awarded the Golden Lion gave us, perhaps, some protection. Now we have President Moon, who is much more sensible and open for actual dialogue.

So it must have been tricky to receive materials from North Korea.

From the very beginning our goal was to invite architects from the North, but it

was very difficult. Later, the Biennale Foundation even sent a letter of invitation to the North requesting their participation – they declined. We had to come up with a Plan B, to which many friends, colleagues, and participating artists from all over the world worked very hard to make it happen. A large part of the materials came from Nick, who was trained as a landscape architect and has been living in China for almost 30 years operating the first tour agency that specializes in trips to Pyongyang. More than anything else, he is a culturally committed and active person. If I could choose who receives the next Nobel Peace Prize, it would be him.

The journey to report the Korean Peninsula started from differences and similarities.

From being one single nation to now a divided land, it was a survey of our similarities and differences through history and architecture, through reflections on both Seoul and Pyongyang as two capital cities. A good example of a literal 'journey' comes from photographer Alessandro Belgiojoso, who had taken two photographs of the border between North and South, as part of a project and publication titled "Korea, an Impossible Journey?" The photos were taken several meters away from each side of the border, but he had to fly from Seoul to Beijing to enter North Korea to take the second photo from a few meters away from the first. Belgiojoso had already exhibited photos from both Koreas prior to our Venice exhibition. I was introduced to him by the former Italian Ambassador to Seoul, Ambassador Mercuri, and was able to invite Belgiojoso to contribute.

There was also a considerable foreign participation and the exhibition had become a common effort.

13 different nations were represented by our participants, each with extensive research or projects regarding Korea, North and South. We were so fortunate to be given the opportunity to represent the Korean Pavilion all together. Beyond the participating artists, there were many behind the scenes contributions. For example, cultural councils from many European nations (the UK, Italy, Germany) with posts in Seoul, with long-standing relationships with the North, were very helpful and active in trying to persuade the North to be involved. [...] MOTOElastico, a Seoul-based architecture firm founded by two Italians, Simone and Marco, participated in the exhibition. They both have really great spirits. Simone always gets around the city on a Vespa and lives in a traditional Korean house. They were so happy that we wanted to present their work as Korean. Their book, Borrowed City, which is about their observations of urban elements in Seoul, and the appropriation of public spaces for private use, in various capacities, was the core of their participation.

Multiplicity Between Art, Architecture and Society

What experiences, in particular, have defined your way in Architecture?

As a child, I was very fond of the classics, arts, and music. I played the piano, which was very important to me. I wanted to see all of the works from the past. My father practiced architecture, but he never pushed me in this direction. I once expressed to him that I wanted to be an artist and he was very supportive. In middle school, I found a book by Le Corbusier on Ronchamp and was so impressed. I thought, "What? Can architects really do this?" My father's office was right below our house, on the ground floor, and there were 20 or 30 people working. I was lucky because it was a very stimulating environment to develop

Previous page
**"Crow's Eye View" Exhibition,
Venice Biennale 2014**
Photo by Hans Jan Dürr

This page
**"Crow's Eye View" Exhibition,
Venice Biennale 2014**
Photos by Jean-Pierre Dalbéra

"Crow's Eye View" Exhibition,
Venice Biennale 2014
Photos by Jean-Pierre Dalbéra

Previous and this page
Korean Pavilion,
Shanghai Expo 2010
Photo by William A.

my passions. I spent hours in the office looking at books and magazines, but my father probably knew that if he told me anything, I would never pursue it! He let me think for myself and I'm only thankful for that. [...] On New Year's Day in 1984, just a year before college, while preparing for the very competitive Korean college entrance exams, I saw Nam June Paik's "Good Morning Mister Orwell" via live satellite TV. He is probably the most famous artist of Korean descent so far. He was a fantastic poet. He was a prophet. He coined the term "electronic superhighway" (1974) which was appropriated by Al Gore 20 years later with the "information superhighway." Paik was a visionary who made us reflect on the progress of technology. In 1982, Paik's "Robot K-456" (Japan, 1964) was unleashed on to the traffic of Madison Avenue in Manhattan and was run over by cars while crossing the street! As I became closer to his works I have always sought out and have been very fortunate to be surrounded by different forms of art and creativity - and that is perhaps why many of my close friends include not just architects, but choreographers, filmmakers, and artists of different disciplines.

Some people may have a hunch that OMA might have been a major influence in your career, but perhaps this is too reductive.

I have 25 years of professional career behind me, but only a tenth of that time has been with OMA. Rem was definitely a strong influence at the time, even before and after, but there have also been and are many other different guided inspirations. While at Columbia for graduate school in the early 90's, I had the rare opportunity to have Kenneth Frampton as a design studio professor. I also took his seminar on Le Corbusier. These two figures were both strong reference points and they have both illuminated me in very significant, yet quite different ways.

Systemic vs Heterogeneous

The context of Seoul inevitably affects an architect's work.

When I returned to Seoul I knew perfectly well that I would have many possibilities. If you consider fellow European and American architects at the time, early 2000's, they had fewer opportunities. Now it's a different situation because Seoul is a post-bubble city. After OMA, I founded a design studio in New York with James Slade, a close friend and a former classmate at Columbia. Together we built the Pixel House which was the first project that gave me an excuse to return to Korea, first temporarily. Then, for a year and a half, there was a sequence of events that led me to relocate permanently. I had never planned to open an office here. From the time I left in the late 80's to my return in 2003, the country transformed from a post-dictatorship state, autocratic and repressive, to a more democratic government with President Roh - there was much progress. Still, initially, I was not inclined to return, but by the time Seoul co-hosted the 2002 World Cup with Japan, there was this new demonstration of young energy and millions of people on the streets in cheerful gatherings - it looked like a whole new nation. It certainly was a challenge, but Korea had changed and evolved. I was willing to take it on, but still knew that I would have to deal with the idiosyncratic conditions that come from such a compressed history and development, resulting in the non-simultaneity of society. [...] I wanted to create an alternative to my previous experiences in New York or Europe and form a certain way of practicing architecture far from the center of discourses and thoughts at the time. In Korea, there's a polarization of two camps. On one side there is the 'systematic' camp, the huge architectural companies which are responsible for 99% of the built environment, who design using a very systematic production. On the other side there is what I call the 'heterogeneous' camp, which consists of smaller studios interested in a certain type of discourse. The first group is very brave, but they feel very guilty because they don't have enough time to get into it and they have just to crank it out - China, for example, has proven quite brave in this aspect. The latter ones are very sensitive, but also very angry because they are seemingly not as involved and cannot create a certain impact, although they are surely quite important to the discourse.

How can you combine the two?

Neither of the two categories is very healthy. I'd like to deal with the 'systematic–heterogeneous' and walk away from both the guilt and anger. That's my formula, as simple as that. Today the situation keeps changing, and thus architecture becomes an inevitable result of multiple variables. If you produce a certain amount of work they begin to create different constellations. You don't want your work to be merely a single answer nor just a passive-reaction to what is given. You can see this in our exhibition "Before/After Mass Studies Does Architecture." Although still developing today, in some ways it was evident in presenting all of our works from the first twelve years. It's like the game of Go: if you are a good player you step ahead because the game is really the result of all of these black and white constellations around you. To win the game you have to be able to look at the bigger picture. At the beginning there was a weird trajectory in the office. We started with small-scaled projects, and just a year later we were designing 100m-tall towers. At the time nobody had taken seriously high-density issues or knew what to do with it.

Some projects have failed, others have been successful and many have transformed. How does one evolve after that?

For 'Before/After' I had two options: I could put all of the models on pedestals - you know, the typical architectural exhibition - showing a specific project from concept to completion, presented through beautiful models and photographs. Instead I took the opportunity for a much deeper research of what my firm had done so far. I asked myself, "What have been our focuses and our preoccupations?" Some of these projects don't even exist anymore, but only survive in the media. For me, architecture is not a goal, and I'm with Cedric Price on that! As a result I've turned down more projects than I've built. [...] Having said that, in the past we have done some really fast projects and more recently some really slow ones. Some were very low-budget and others very expensive. As a result of capitalism, usually the bigger-faster-cheaper go together. You might think that bigger projects take more time but it's actually quite the opposite. The 2010 Shanghai Expo Korea Pavilion was perhaps the main bigger-faster-cheaper project, and an extreme case. It was one of our first overseas projects, so we put a lot of energy into it - even though the budget was reduced and it had to be demolished shortly after. For an earlier project, the client had completely changed the direction of the project midway - as if producing a serious film and suddenly having to turn it into a comedy. We still had a lot of fun with the project, and today it has a completely different identity and function. In recent years I've become very skeptical about these types of short-lived projects. Now with more experience, I'm more for longer-lasting things - I think all of my latest projects show this kind of attitude. They are projects that live longer and even age well over time. I try not to be wasteful and take full advantage of the opportunity.

This and next page
Boutique Monaco
Photo by Fernando Herrera

Now the developers are looking at the city as a living environment and no longer as cheap stock.

South Korea is at the peak of our population and from now on it can only decrease very quickly, becoming a demographic situation like Europe. The role of architecture will have to change inevitably, and it is already heading towards that direction. The 2008 crisis was one of those breaking points. If you look at Japan, at the beginning of the 90s, there was the so-called 'post-bubble generation.' Here instead we have the 'post-2008 generation.' Now, city-making is no longer about easy money. Now we are more concerned about making the city for the human experience. Korea has been one of the most severe cases of an economy driven by construction. That's why everything looks the same. When you look at stock you don't care about the designer of the stock right? Even before this I started doing architecture with a certain long-lasting agenda. Projects have a generous time frame and have assumed a much more important role.

The Double Gaze

The crisis had passed but the constraints of FAR regulations still remain. Now new possibilities are arising thanks to this kind of new attitude of clients. It seems now is a revolutionary time to look for the breakthroughs and fresh ways to generate a new positive discourse. Several architects are divided between Koreanness, materiality, creating a link with history and observing the society defining a certain spatial logic. Do you think Korean architects have some responsibilities?

I hear this question a lot. Many well-informed Western architects reiterate this aspect and ask me about it quite often. But, for example, what would you answer if I asked you, "What is the Italianness to you? To the architecture you do?" What would you say? So why do Koreans have to answer this? Thinking of the Japanese, they did it so well. They spoke of nature and purity, but they have been alongside the Modernists from the very beginning, for over 100 years, and have been an active participant in the dialogue of Modernism with the West, influencing one another. For the latecomers like Korea, who have not been a part of this early dialogue in the modern period, I'd say there is a self-conscious attitude to the 'double gaze.' It's a kind of psyche that describes the way we act when we don't present ourselves through our own gaze but through that of others, often passively. We present ourselves in a different way because we are aware of the others. I always thought this was very defensive. For me, without this historic baggage, it's necessary to tackle different and emerging conditions at the same time. To be fair, I'm not sure how to summarize them yet or if I even should because of this. Also in this global context, because often architects develop their own identity and quickly become almost like a brand - people ask you to do the same thing again and again. In terms of branding, Mass Studies has been the most unwise because we completely avoid it. In fact, I am still very much interested in exploring each of the given concrete realities. I want to use my architectural practice as an investigation to understand what has happened and what is happening here and beyond, all at the same time.

This and next page
Boutique Monaco
Photo by Fernando Herrera

This and previous page
Daum Space.1
Photo by Jang Jin-wook

This and previous page
Daum Space.1
Photo by Jang Jin-wook

We believed that to improve our situation, we had to design "not conventionally right" or with undefinable approaches... I focus on studying the situation in Seoul, the problems of each district and trying to understand new design strategies of which we still do not have a reference. I invite all architects interested in this direction to design here.

Kim Young-joon
YO2 Architects

Not Only One Direction
Repetition as an Evolving Approach
Life In-Between Spaces
Design Layout vs Program
Initiative Consideration to Generate the Design
Not Telling People What to Do
Not Conventionally Right

Kim Young-joon Interview
Photo by the author

[...] I have never looked only at the Korean architectural panorama, but I always tried to start from a much broader sense of understanding. My first job, as a fresh graduate, was working as an editor for the magazine "Space Group". It was an experience that shaped my point of view on architecture, making me look at the world scene rather than local fashion or a specific taste. [...] In the 80s, it was the moment of the architectural identity debate. People were struggling to establish a link between tradition and modernity, asking themselves: "What is Koreaness in Architecture?"—We have to keep in mind it was the period of the dictatorship of Park Chung Hee and Chun Doo Hwan and, as all dictators do, they were focused on finding a tool to give a substantial impact to the society. All professionals were affected, and all architects and developers established a similar way of doing. From Seoul to the entire country, the architecture became a literal translation from tradition to modernity. [...] My situation was unique. All members of the committee at "Space Group" were architects who had trained overseas - my older generation - and they were setting the basis for a different architectural debate.

Not Only One Direction

[...] In the mid-90s, I got fascinated by the book "Delirious New York"... I was a young architect and thoroughly fascinated by ideas coming from overseas. So I began to read all the treaties and essential books written by Western theorists. Inevitably I had to seek something outside, and I was pushed to go far away from Korea. [...]

What was a significant difference between Europe and Seoul?

Living abroad it is always exciting, and sometimes you understand things, or you ask questions you had never thought possible before. So I learned from living and experiencing cultures and languages and converting them into experiences and spaces, uses and programs... Let's say, I was learning from architecture itself. [...] I moved to London first, to study at the Architectural Association, and later I worked for OMA in Rotterdam. I think I grasped the ideas neither from the university nor the office... I have been studying the texts by Rem Koolhaas, and I decided to learn as much as I could about all the new approaches to urbanism and architecture. I tried to collect the Western concepts from history and contemporary practices as well as experiencing and visiting Europe. [...] My reading and researching were the most effective teachers for me, and I understood one of the most important lessons: in our profession, there is no perfect style or particular direction we can take.

How did this inclusive conclusion shape your way of designing?

[...] My opinion is outside from conventional architecture... At the beginning I started by observing the city and the urbanism, developing an idea of "global architecture" that goes beyond a single building. My design became focused on an architectural philosophy which can shift closer to the urbanism theory and can revolutionize the direction of the design, from urbanism to architecture.

Repetition as an Evolving Approach

The 80s was the time of the architectural debate, but when I came back it was already 1998, and new approaches were applied massively to the architectural scene. If you look at Europe and the conceptualization of the context after the

ZWKM
Photo by Kim Jae-kyeong

reconstruction after World War II, the approaches were based on escaping from alienation and repetitions. [...] When I was in Europe, I realized architects were trying to build heterogeneous architecture but, once in Seoul, I comprehended that here the situation was different. The context was formed by a mix of small-scale, old *Hanoks*, Japanese architecture of the 30s invaded by real estate mega developments, and contemporary small buildings at the side of mega-structures... extremely chaotic. That is why we needed more homogeneous things here.

In the past, many issues of European cities were caused by a blind repetition of typologies, which originated degradation and alienation. In the future, what is the solution to avoid the same problem in Seoul?

The little book 'Collective Form', by Fumihiko Maki, can become handy in these cases. In the past, it had a significant influence on my ideas and offered me a clue to achieve complexity in buildings. [...] It is not merely freeing from alienation issues, but creating architecture related to the users and contemporary conditions. In the 60s, Maki's society was requesting big scale projects to power the growth. So he proposed 'Collective Forms' as the solution to the bigness and an answer for the growing demand of the time. His solution was an architecture created by replicating and splitting large structures to build a combination of sub-systems... I worked on these concepts, and I have been focusing on repetitions and comprehending the relationship between program and space. My work continued exploring the possibilities given by the process of division and reorganization of functions to generate structures and masses... It is not only repetition but a differentiated repetition. It is what I call an "evolving approach"; an evolutionary method where the repetition evolves, creating changes. This idea can be implemented to generate architecture systems composed of levels, both expanding horizontally and vertically, well fitted to the high-density cities like Seoul. [...] We can create architecture according to a "Composite Masses" theory—I carry out this idea primarily into house design, but I also extended it to various typologies. First, this notion is based on divisions conforming to programs and specific conditions which can be either more public or private. Second, I consider the program characters and make their proper consistencies and combinations.

How do you practically combine these masses and what are the effects on the urban landscape?

You know, a specific density, like here in Seoul, has limitations. We cannot develop a wider variety of formal solutions. Architecture has to be compact. Then, the matter is about how we incorporate the groups with a specific composition inside the building boundaries... The real issue is: "How are you going to support and extend the urban character of the previous or existing street-scape?". In all my works you can see connections from the public ground level to the upper floors to create other public areas in various levels of the building—this also becomes an architectural language to solve the characters of some parts of the exterior. [...]

Life In-Between Spaces

Since the establishment of the MAT archetype, the system had moments of glory and decline. Your projects are reviving mega-structural ideas and all-encompassing principles... How do you update the model to contemporary

Hakhyunsa Model
Photo by Kim Jae-kyeong

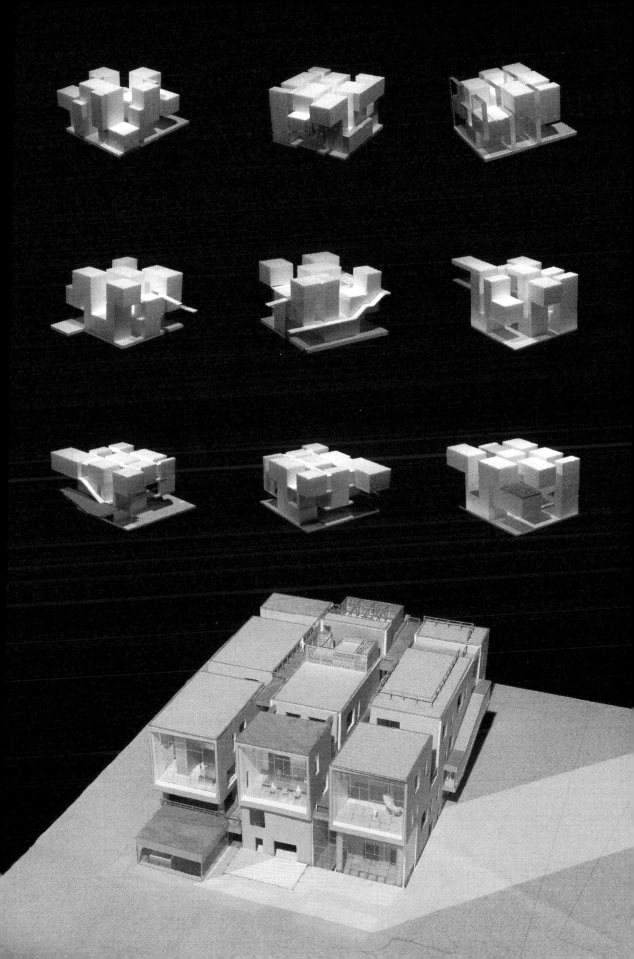

knowledge and modern way of life?

[...] I developed further the statutory scheme of the MAT. When I visited Freie University in Berlin, all the courtyards did not seem particularly characteristic. However, since the project is on a hilly site, it adapts and transforms according to the various levels. So you can see that, even if the structure is simple, it creates an interesting phenomenon of slight changes. My architecture is alike. I am making similar spaces but always trying slightly different spatial compositions. The key factor for achieving diversity is to intervene in the relationship played by the solid and the voids. From these two different conditions you can affect characters and qualities; the more you develop the project, the more you can create complexity in the design.

Design Layout vs Program

[...] We have to understand that even houses—like architecture—could have unique programs. This functions might be unexpected and go far beyond straightforward uses. In fact, housing projects can relate to other unrelated functions like teaching, working and even meditation. Operating divisions between the programs, I create zones of a structural and systematic mix, which can generate a different system of relationships. This involves interior and exterior connections creating zones of unpredicted potential... I am fascinated by space in-between the buildings which generally we abandon, or we consider as outside. For instance, there might be spaces in-between the dining and the living room that typically are connected by a particular functional indoor space. Instead, I would create outdoor areas intermediating those programs. [...] In a city is like in a house, the critical things are in-between the functions. The scale does not change my approach; I keep the same idea. When you design from an urbanistic understanding, you cannot see the building as a single self-standing structure - one of the main problems of contemporary Korean cities. My starting idea is to rethink, rebuild, and reorganize the design across all scales, creating continuity and breaking the boundaries between the architecture and the city. What I like to call it is "urbanism for architecture" approach - but it works as well the way around, "architecture for urbanism". It is a powerful tool envisioned already by several architects before me, but not yet effectively implemented in our contexts.

Initiative Consideration to Generate the Design

What is the starting point of your design process?

My first step is to begin by separating and then recollecting. Different from my colleagues, this approach cannot be elaborated by sketches. I am diagrammatic, which implies developing many alternatives, approaching the design only little by little until the final result. With this procedure, you do not create shapes but systematic solutions, so what comes next cannot be defined as "formal solution". I always say that the mere shape generates a system in which constructions compete among themselves; no positive effect can come out of it. My goal is not to make photographic architecture, but to craft organisms. I constantly ask myself "What is the formless architecture?". When I design, I keep it in mind, and I make an envelope as simple as possible. [...] From history, typically, we have always considered the elevation only a projection of what is inside the building. However, if you reverse this concept, the indoor program

Top Page
ZWKM Model
Courtesy of Yo2 Architects

Bottom page
ZWKM Bird-eye view
Photo by Kim Jae-kyeong

can be changed by the structure of the pattern - the different size of windows, connections between outside and inside - and paths wrapping the volume. So my design starts from the outside, and it expands to the inside.

Not Telling People What to Do

[...] We are living in a fast society, based on consumerist mentality. People have the wrong assumption that photos on the magazines are representing the final architectural state. However, after the completion, people are changing everything. Inside a structural system, space can change and the users will not need to transform an architecture radically, but the arrangement will allow easy small changes. That is why I do not consider myself an actor but only an audience of the constant shifting state of the architecture.

In this way, space is created to prepare future programs not yet considered.

Take Adolf Loos. He was not satisfied in designing only space, he designed clothes too, intending to define an entire way of life of his clients. So what can we get from forcing what we propose on the people? When you see the urban scale, you cannot control every aspect of the urban living, but still, you need to intervene. [...] Our work is to ask ourselves "What is fixed and what is unfixed in Architecture?".

Not Conventionally Right

Everybody tells us that we are moving too fast, demolishing large parts of our remaining legacy and building too many big real estate developments. I remember my childhood years; we were in an unfortunate situation. You cannot imagine how much has changed! However, in early 2000, the society started regretting the loss. We destroyed all the memories, and only a few things survived from the life we experienced. People now are trying to discover a way to go back and seeking to live in a certain equilibrium. [...]

How is your dream city like?

Balance is the most important thing. We have to create something for what we lost. We need to prepare for the future; a future of what we cannot find any reference from existing condition all over the world - from a particular point of view, East and West are facing this together. I believe we need to recover some aspects of the past, but we cannot make Seoul a historical city like Milan, that can only result from a long historical stratification... Here it is lost. At the same time, we cannot erase everything which had been accumulated in the last 50 years, because all the new actions have to start from the current situation and to upgrade it for our necessities.

Seoul is a high-density city. If 'erasing' is not an option, then how do you achieve that goal?

I am working as a City Architect of Seoul. We are trying to change the system in various directions. For instance, no more super-high-rise and huge real estate developments. The new Seoul has to be different. Our role is to decide the direction of architecture according to the reality. What is needed, in the Korean situation, is not to build on new virgin lands. In Seoul city, we do not have enough spaces to develop more. That means we have to generate architecture from an inner development point of view. When density is getting higher, you need to consider

Top Page
Sajik Park Artwork Model
Courtesy of Yo2 Architects

Bottom page
Sajik Park Artwork
Photo by Kim Jae-kyeong

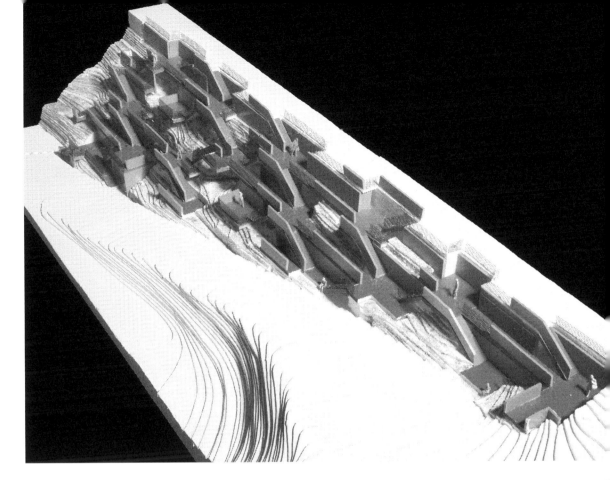

Seoguipo Residence
Photo by Kim Jae-kyeong

different architectural solutions which sometimes can intervene or penetrate the existing system.

How would you define this new approach out of the existing condition?

[...] When I was in the Netherlands in the mid-90s, at OMA we had the strategy to create always new solutions. We believed that for improving our situation, we needed to design approaches "not conventionally right", or not definable... Like the newly built Skyway project in Seoul by MVRDV [Seoullo 7017]. Now you could ask me "How do you categorize this design? Is it architecture, landscape or a civil engineering structure?". It is not definable because is a mixed design, coming from different backgrounds. This approach is required to fix our environment. [...] My focus is on studying the Seoul situation, the problems of each district, and trying to understand new design strategies of which we do not have any reference yet. I am inviting all the architects interested in this direction to design here. [...] If we look at the long run, I am pragmatic, and I find solutions based on the reality of our cities.

Top Page
Seoguipo Residence
Courtesy of YO2 Architects

Bottom Page
Seoguipo Residence
Photo by Kim Jae-kyeong

Top Page
Taekwongo Park Model
Courtesy of Y02 Architects

The "Universal Space" frees us from the burden of finding a solution for specific functions, making it possible to return to the original raison d'être of architecture. Buildings can be machines, but it's more than that: by becoming free we can emancipate from the burden of functionality...We are looking to the future, but somehow it is linked to our old past.

Hwang Doo-jin
Doojin Hwang Architects

Missing Context
Taking from the Past
User Spatial Expectation
Old Hanoks, New Hanoks
Korean, Japanese, and Chinese
Beyond Program

Hwang Doo-jin Interview
Photo by the author

Missing Context

[...] The last surviving residential buildings in Seoul were built in the late 19th century. What it means is that whatever was here before was all destroyed. That's remarkable!

How do you design in such a context?

We are trapped in between. Different from Europe, there is not much history left. It doesn't seem that we have an anchor to start with but here is not like Arizona... so we don't start completely from Tabula Rasa. We are not dealing with history per se, but you're not handling with untouched nature either. It's an awkward situation in between. So here we have to be careful if you want to do sensitive architecture. There is something you can completely ignore but there are other things you have to take into consideration. If you look at the city, from the design point of view, you will be a bit disappointed. But if you seek in terms of how a city works, this is an interesting city. In this habitat one building depends on another, even if it seems that they don't have any connection.

How do you start a project and how do you consider the complexity of this situation?

That's a good question. I guess I have a specific way of dealing with situations like this. I am starting with what is there now because I think the current situation matters the most. Then I do some historical research to find out if there are some interesting elements, any important elements I should incorporate into my design. Sometimes I am successful, but even if I'm not, I don't try hard to invent any contraption because I feel it is a silly thing to do.

Taking from the Past

[...] For example, where we are now is my home, and my office. If you open that door you could enter my residence. It's a mixed-use building.

So you never take a break from work?

Yes, I do. When I first started living like this, I had health problems because I never stopped. Now I know how to control myself. I've been living like this for the last 15 years and now living close to my work is okay. For example, when we moved here we continued to do little things to develop this building. This part of the building is new [private office of the architect], which we extended in 2010 but the other part of the building is 40-years-old. Since we did some works on this property, we took the opportunity to connect the main street next to the royal palace to small alleys inside the urban block. I realized it was an interesting urban texture, and a very monumental environment. Traditionally there had been nothing that connected the two. This was more for the royal family than for the ordinary people. I hoped this land could be used as a visual connection between the two. So what I did it was knocking down the existing wall and replaced it with a trellis wall to see through. I thought it was very important to bridge the gap and to connect two radically different urban contexts. That's what was already here and what I wanted to add was based on whatever I found in history. They are usually just small things or sometimes little details. When we first moved here, the main building was painted in white as it is now. I seriously considered about repainting it in a different color. Then I learned the traditional concept of colors in different

Castle of Skywalkers
Photo by Park Young-chac

directionalities. The center is yellow - that's the color the Chinese Emperor used to wear, their golden robes to represent the center of power. South is purple, north is black, east is blue, and the west is white. Here the color white was just a coincidence. It is a modern house and probably who designed and built it had none of the understanding of our traditional concepts. So that's why we kept the color white here. But personally, it is quite fun because we have a lot of things to play with, which are contemporarily existing conditions. But sometimes if you want, you can go back to history and find something interesting from the past.

User Spatial Expectation

How do you compose the architecture and the interior design?

Interestingly it all depends... but in most cases, you have to start to understand how to maximize the area and the scale. Here it is crowded and we have a strange building code so we just try to figure out what the envelope would be. Then it boils down to finding out a clue for the design. Occasionally if you had an actual good view or a specific direction of the property, it could give you a lot of clues. It's not like designing a building in a desert here is loaded with context. But if we get out in the countryside, we no longer need to be bothered by little things. I actually found it quite interesting that in these situations I became increasingly dependent on geometry. Because geometry is a self-referential clue for a lot of what we do as architects. But only up to a certain limit because I don't believe in free form in architecture because it actually gives you a uniform experience. I like the DDP [Dongdaemun Design Plaza by Zaha Hadid Architects] and I admire it from any different point of view. But the spatial experience you receive from the building is quite uniform. On the other hand, when you have a better playing with the geometries the building starts to reveal intricacies as you explore within it. That is exactly what I try to do normally.

It is the exploration of space that creates an expectation for users. How do you create and give a quality to space?

I'm more inclined towards creating an experience rather than forms. Formal aspects of architectural design are always interesting, but I'm more interested in creating a situation in which a different experience can take place. For example, we have a reputation that no matter what buildings we design they all end up being party houses. [Laughs]. We believe in playing with a close connection between the outside and the inside and, with a weather pattern like in Korea, if a building has a great relationship between the interior and exterior it easily becomes a party place. People love those buildings... this office also is an excellent place and we give parties here! It has a lot of qualities given by the connections. Visual penetration is something we'd like to achieve. I'm a firm believer in the Piranesian space; I think it's a wonderful thing. You can feel something larger than the space you physically occupy, creating the sense of connectedness and the sense of contrast between different scales of space.... The concept of the Piranesian space is of course western. Piranesi was Italian, but it doesn't necessarily mean that historically we don't have the conception here. Indeed, we do and when I found that out, I felt it was interesting and compelling and then I fell in love with the idea of working with traditional Korean buildings. For example, in Korean traditional architecture, the living quarters are created by post and beam structure based on the orthogonal grid system. But the roof of traditional Korean buildings has a saddle surface which is 3-dimensionally curved. Usually, these two geometries cannot go together very well so to make them work we have a third structure that works as a mediator between the two. It's when a higher-level carpentry comes into play. Working with this geometry of a building is a fascinating idea for me and I've been trying to do that in many of our projects. By doing that, what we can achieve is creating buildings in which the spatial experiences keep changing no matter where you are located. Because the geometries, the different type of geometries, can meet one and another unexpectedly and that gives you pleasure of exploring the space, making you appreciate to be in a special kind of building. I don't know how much you know but I have a reputation in Korea of being a typical contemporary architect who has continuously been engaged in designing new traditional *Hanoks*. One thing I've learned from the process of working on traditional Korean buildings is that the main point is not just about a physical building but the principle behind it. *Hanok* is a wonderful example of Asian Piranesian space. We have a lot of visual penetrations and also we have a great a juxtaposition of many types of geometry. When we build the corner of the roof the rafters radiate like a fan and from the carpenter's point of view, it is extremely difficult to make each piece. For whatever reason, our ancestors adopted the system and continue to use it even for ordinary houses. For me porosity and layered geometry are the key concepts essential to my work as a contemporary architect... Do you play music? This is a rough comparison, but if we compare architecture to music, the Korean traditional architecture is like jazz. If you look at jazz music, there is nothing much in it. They have this thing called the Real Book with a collection of famous jazz music. That is what musicians look up when they play jazz music. They improvise. That exact note does not really matter but if you study typical classical music everything is written. Some composers like to make sure that the performer makes no interpretation. In Korean traditional architecture, it is nothing like that, but it includes a lot of improvisation.

Old Hanoks, New Hanoks

It's rare. Even other Asian architects I interviewed over the years never built a traditional house from scratch... At most, they added a few new things.

I understand that this Korean situation is quite unique... This idea is more like an experimental thing. I always wonder why we should cover the roof of *Hanoks* with clay tiles? Why couldn't it be done with glass? What the structure can do is to give you a great sense of light and shadow. This is my response to Mies van der Rohe's glass skyscraper in 1922. The building looks the best when there is just the skeleton but, when you start to clad it, it loses its beauty. Why do we do the same thing with our traditional architecture? This was an engineering nightmare because no one had done it before!

Did you receive any critics?

A lot of critics! I usually answer with a kind of provocation.... My *Hanok* practice should be divided into two different groups: one is the process which I call "creative restoration", and the second one is when you create something completely new. Yet another possibility is to get inspiration from *Hanok* and apply the principles to contemporary buildings. Everybody in a certain way does that... not just in Korea but also in Japan, in Europe and America, the tradition sometimes plays a deep role. Mostly the provocation comes for the second group of work. My response is that in every civilized country traditional buildings do not die but they keep evolving. For some reasons in this country that historical evolution took

Fazio House
Phoenix Springs Country Club 15
Photo by Park Young-chae

Fazio House
Phoenix Springs Country
Club 32
Photo by Park Young-chae

place for an incredibly short period of time. I think somebody has to do it, so it's just a matter of responding to the demand of the society. People continue to live in those houses and you cannot just leave those people with whatever shitty buildings they own. So it's imperative that we should upgrade the system of the building. It should be livable from the 21st-century lifestyle perspective. This is beyond discussion; it has to be done! Somebody has to do it and I've been doing it. With the third group, creating something different and new with the traditional system, I pushed the wooden framework further. In this way I could create much slenderer and much lighter structures than the very typical Korean traditional roof. As a contemporary architect I like the proportion of the very slender steel pieces and glass buildings but when I look at *Hanoks* everything looks extremely heavy. From the structural point of view, it's over-designed. What I wanted to do is to come up with something lighter. This can be done for instance, by creating a sandwich beam with metal plates in the middle and wood pieces on both sides. At the same time, the wood pieces would work as a fire insulation. If you study the proportion, it's something unheard-of. Some people might not be happy with things like that. But you know, we need to experiment.

I believe most of the critics are coming from people from the west or with a western background.

That's right.

In the past, in Asian architecture, all the materials were constantly fixed and replaced... different from the West.

That's a good point. The masonry buildings are associated with western architecture and they can preserve it... our wooden structure would not be expected to last that long. So we are much familiar with this concept of rebuilding by disassembling and substituting the old parts with something new. That's part of our heritage. For example, the South Gate of Seoul, our number one national treasure was burnt by fire caused by a madman. We completely rebuilt it and the people say this is no longer original but, as a matter of fact, the burnt one had been heavily rebuilt over and over. So what do you mean by original? Even if you see UNESCO's Nara Documents, with wooden structure buildings it's okay to use new elements, as long as the design is authentic. So our concept is based on a sort of evolution.

Korean, Japanese, and Chinese

What are the differences between traditional architecture from Korea, Japan, and China?

I have been trying to answer this question since I was in college. Later when I was practicing architecture people too were asking this question... I guess it is that attitude towards nature, as well as scale and materiality. In Korea, we tend to believe that in China they imitate nature too much. They are masters of creating nature that looks very artificial. If you see the garden from a Korean perspective, you think: "You guys are doing too much!"; but if you go to Japan, they make everything abstract. For us, it looks great and we appreciate it but for the Koreans eyes, both sound artificial. So in Korea, the concept we like the most is an artificial nature that looks so natural that cannot be distinguished from the real one. In this way, we bridge the gap between the very concept of artificiality and naturality. If you go to the Changdeok Palace and the secret garden [Huwon] behind it, you see

This and next page
Tongin Market Art Gate
Photos by Park Young-chae

Chunwon Party
Photos by Park Young-chae

it is actually one of the most popular tourist attractions. There you have that the garden which is just a forest with the buildings scattered in it. It doesn't seem like a garden, but all the plants were artificially planted. In terms of materiality, I guess Chinese don't seem like being happy with just one sense of materiality but they keep adding things to it. In Japan instead, they torture material until it completely gives up. I assume we should let things be what they are. It is incredibly difficult to tell the differences you know, we are walking into a thick air.

Sometimes with some simplifications, you can tackle complicated issues.

Yes, I mean, like French architecture or Italian architecture. Probably you can tell the differences or sometimes you might just shake your head; am I saying the right thing? Getting back to where we were, China was an empire that assumed it was at the center of the world. The Chinese scale from our Korean perspective is exaggerated. Many buildings don't feel like they were built for human beings. I mean you see imperial attitude and grandeur into it. Back in Japan, they are much into making everything diminutive, sometimes even more diminutive than human scale. What I appreciate the most about Korean traditional architecture is this close relationship between building and your body.... Koreans are now 15 cm taller than they were a hundred years ago. We are the fastest growing people in all Asian. But even these days when we visit traditional houses, the best thing is that the building looks like it's inviting you to take a certain posture. Like when you lay down, and the window is also located down so you can see outside, looking at this beautiful view of the mountains. From my point of view, Korean traditional houses were never meant to be a permanent shelter, as the western houses were. It was more like a tent. I sometimes go out camping and staying inside the tent I have the same impression... I consider it important for us to feel the changes in the weather when we are inside. We like to listen to the rain and we even like to listen to the sound of the snow falling; it doesn't seem possible, but it is. The sense of connectivity between you and what is outside is the core issue of the value of Korean traditional architecture. Normally when we do projects, and when we talk to our clients, I try to use not too much rhetoric because my skin starts to crawl. So I try to use commonsensical, ordinary terms but nothing rhetorical... If I convey my ideas better in this way, there is no reason I should not be doing it.

Beyond Program

It's interesting to see how so far you haven't explained your architecture through the program.

Because function... as I practice architecture more, I realized I have become less and less dependent on this fixed concept of functions. I expect eventually architecture, I don't know especially when, to become something like a chameleon. The function and the program of the building will keep changing as time passes by. A café in the morning can be a classroom in the afternoon and it can be home at night. All these wonderful technological advancements in the world and all the gadgets, utensils and the appliances we use, they are getting smaller and smaller and sometimes they are invisible. They occupy little space and they don't have a formalistic impact on the building we design. It's the demise of Modernism. Functionalism we have been doing for a long time is a fading thing because the formalistic aspect of the modern architecture was a direct response to the Machine Age. At the time all these machines were crude, so they required a specific formalistic approach to make them work. The library is a good example.

This and next page
Chunwon Party
Photos by Park Young-chae

When you enter the main hall there were a series of card boxes but these days you just look at a single box on the computer screen. You type in and it exactly tells you where the book is. This invisibility of high-tech gadgets is a key factor in bringing *Hanoks* back to us. In the old days, when I was a student, we learned at school it was okay to study *Hanoks* and to get some inspiration from it. But we were told not to work on it because it was dead. In retrospect, the *Hanok* started to come back, sometimes at the beginning of the millennia, exactly when small gadgets like Wi-Fi, home security system and things like that became popular, easy and accessible. When working on our first few *Hanoks* it seemed like magic. There are a lot of cavities in the building and you can put all these things inside without changing its forms. It became a fully wired building with all the modern appliance we need for the 21th-century lifestyle! I realize that whatever modernism we had known for a long time, it's gone and now it's the next chapter, dealing with the situation in which technology is far more advanced compared to the time of Le Corbusier and Mies van der Rohe. If Mies came back, he would find everything much more relevant now. I'm sure because in his time it was not possible to completely solve the problem of sound, thermal and waterproofing but we know it is possible now. Now we have unidirectional microphones and speakers and everything that instantly changes a place from the classroom into something else. In Mies' time, the concept was there, it is amazing that he came up with the concept, but technically the society in the 1950s and 60s was not advanced enough... So as a matter of fact, our office is in the process of completely re-designing our homepage and the number one question is how to group our projects. You normally group your projects on the concept of program like office, residential, etc. But most of what we design these days is mixed-use buildings. There is not a single category program that covers them so how can we define it? That's probably why the book "S. M. L, XL" came out. This is a more convenient way of grouping. The method we have come up with was to create "filters" with themes like porosity, layered geometry, and those filters can go on top of this functional grouping. It is difficult because we are living in a transient period for functionality and program of architecture. In Korean traditional architecture, one room can play all different things depending on what you do. If you eat there, it becomes a dining room, if you sleep there it becomes a bedchamber and if you work on something it becomes your study. That is an extreme flexibility in terms of the way we use spaces, so we are not new to this. It's already familiar.

How would you be designing the Mies' "Universal Space", with the present situation, technologies and taking into account 80 years' critics?

The "Universal Space", actually it will free us from the burden of coming up with a solution for specific functions of the room and it makes it even possible for us to go back to the original raison d'être of a building. Why do we build? I guess we build because the building is the mediator between us, human beings, and nature. So buildings can be a machine, but it's more than that. So, by becoming freer, and liberated from the burden of functionality, we can focus more on the space, the physicality of the architecture, the sensory aspect of space and structure. That pushes us back to where we were a long time ago, even in the prehistoric time. This is challenging and exciting. We are looking at the future but somehow the future is related to our old past.

This and next page
The Bricks
Photos by Park Young-chae

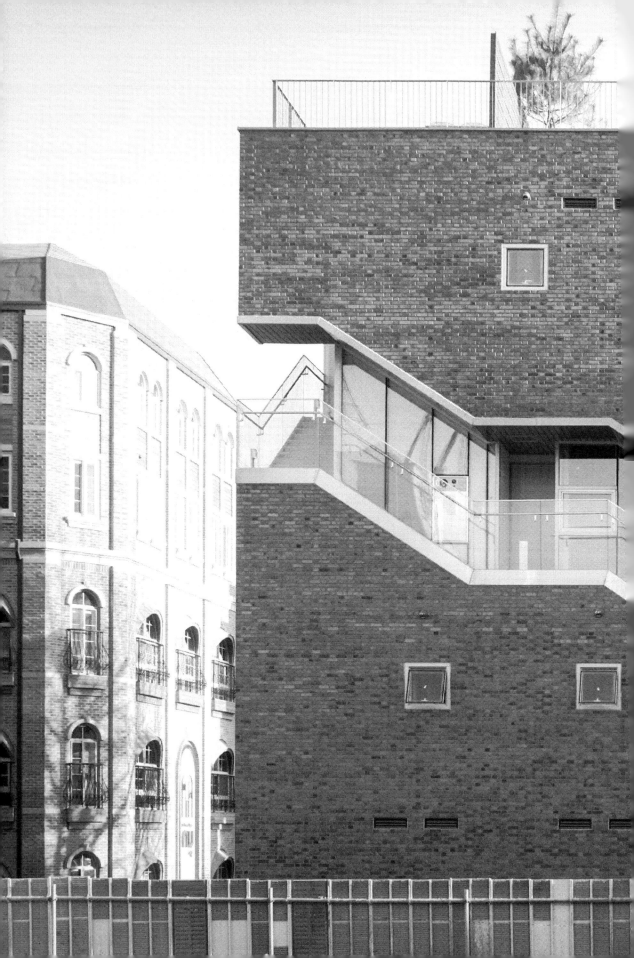

The West Village
Photos by Park Young-chae

Won & Won 63.5
Photos by Kim Yong-kwan

Won & Won 63.5
Photo by Kim Yong-kwan

I believe that space should flow. The closed space is a dead space; to give vitality to a space, it must be opened. We must create connections with the natural environment... Traditionally we say: "putting buildings on the ground". We do not occupy the ground with architecture, but we "borrow space from nature".

Kim In-cheurl
Archium

Learning from Tradition
Space In-between
Practical Tradition
Floor Area Ratio
4.3 Group

Kim In-cheurl Interview
Photo by the author

Learning from Tradition

In the past, we received only the concepts coming from modern architecture, and we studied and followed the Western model for almost a century, producing today's city . But now it's finally changing. Yes, Modernism is the basis of our condition, but now we are learning to use also old ideas derived from the tradition. Several architects, like myself, are interpreting many inherited concepts, bringing them back to the present. [...] Somehow I am essentially a Korean architect, I didn't study overseas... I started working in the field of architecture back in 1965. At that time, the level of the university was not sufficient... yes, there were some qualified professors, but they were not architects. It is essential to have professors who also practice to have a broader understanding of the discipline, and to receive practical experience. So I learned architecture from a rather technological and engineering point of view. [...]

Were there any turning moments at the beginning? How did you define the trajectory of your architecture?

In the 1970s, there was a strong wave of industrialization here in Korea. Many architects were very busy building square meters over square meters, but I must say that "architecture" - in a critical sense - did not exist. Irritated by this situation, I had begun to study in depth what architecture is, and at the end of the 90s I showed the findings in my first exhibition in Tokyo. After this, I realized that it was essential for me to come back and redefine the basis of the architectural discipline, so I took our tradition as a teacher... Culture, artifacts, and our natural environment have become my masters, guiding my agenda and what I would become as an architect and person.

What was the main lesson you've learned?

The traditional Korean architecture gave me mainly a different way to consider the building envelope. Historic buildings are not based on a masonry structure but a framework. This system consists of a free floor, an independent structure, and empty walls filled or closed up with light materials. Strangely, they look exactly like the features described in the five principles of Le Corbusier's architecture. But unlike these principles, in our traditional architecture, there is no limit between what is inside and outside. Space is then controlled and defined by frames, not by structures. All concepts used in my architecture derive from tradition... although my buildings seem rather contemporary, they have strong traditional roots. When I start a project, I always try to understand the connection between inside and outside, looking for all the potential links... I begin taking the hypothetical mass and look at the possible surrounding relationships. [...]

Space In-between

[...] In the past, our ancestors did not have a closed architecture, but it was part of something larger... In traditional philosophy, humans are part of nature. Thus the architecture became the mediator between these two realms.

How do you design the edge in between the inside and outside?

I believe that space should flow. The closed space is a dead space; to give the vitality to a space, it must be opened. [...] In architecture, we must create connections with the natural environment... In the traditional architecture

language, we say: "putting buildings on the ground". We do not occupy the ground with architecture, but we use the idea of "borrowing space from nature". It follows that we must not create a barrier from nature.

How can we translate this traditional concept into contemporary architecture?

It differs from a shape or a style, but that is the power to create concepts and ideas for contemporary architecture, translating the traditional way into a new way... For example, Gangnam's Urban Hive Building is a very contemporary building, as a dynamic space and for its dimensions. The traditional idea behind the project is the peculiarity of the structure. The supporting structure is outside, and in between the structure and the architectural space, you can see an interface, creating the connection to the city. I always try to dismantle the boundary of architectural space and create spaces in between the edge, bridging the link between the two worlds.

Practical Tradition

They can be physical or visual connections...

Yes, they can be done in different ways, but they must create a unified space. The boundary of the building is not "real" but is just an imaginary line on a map or a drawing. The skin of the building is the main element, creating unity between inside and outside, and this architectural element is the one that I care the most about when designing. This can act through a physical limit or a limit of visual perception. There can be so many ways to play with!

In practice, how does this limit works?

For example, if you use a wall, you will enclose the space, but if you use a porous frame, it opens the space, creating connections and characters. In the Kim Ok-Gil [Memorial Hall Project] it is evident, and this project is one of my first that used this concept. [...] The site area has quite influenced the design solution. The trapezoidal-shaped plot defined a building with a very narrow side. This issue could have created a very claustrophobic environment. Looking at the photos, you can see how this was avoided. I created a volume that would give a feeling of openness, building virtual but very active extensions of the space. The appearance of the interior is defined by a sequence of reinforced concrete elements, overlapping without touching each other, and with an ample space between them. [...] The details are interesting: the windows do not have a support structure, and they don't cast shadows. This gives the illusion that there is not even glass to separate the concrete beams... If we look at the traditional wooden structure, we see that it is the same thing. In traditional architecture, the supporting structure is external. In the space between the structure and the thin-walled membrane, there is a specific space that can accommodate various functions. As you can see, there are two layers: a porous virtual surface defined by the structure and a thin one of light mobile elements. This is the difference between the western bearing wall, consisting of a single layer, and the Korean wall, formed by a sequence of elements. If we think of the Korean climate, we see that it has four well-defined seasons from 30 ° C to -30 ° C. This specific situation is the architectural condition in Korea. Traditionally, we never tried to artificially change the internal climate conditions because we wanted to perceive nature and the changing of seasons. Today, even if we have technologies that can alter the internal climate, we still always try to recreate this spatial composition.

Next, this, and previous page
Persona
Courtesy of Archium

This and previous page
Memorial
Courtesy of Archium

Floor Area Ratio

There are extreme architectural and urban restrictions, but I don't think they are a terrible condition for us... Instead, I believe it is a condition that pushes our work forward. Each building is influenced by what is around it. So, regulations are relevant because, although the architecture is privately owned, it is an issue that affects the city and the community. Buildings cannot exist individually; they are an integral part of the public realm.

How do you explore the possibilities with these restrictions?

[...] I feel lucky because it's a constant challenge for me. The FAR is very useful and a critical aspect of my projects. With FAR, I can automatically generate the form and distribution of the unit. However, we must be able to understand the situation, to reformulate, revolutionizing the limits of the urban environment... In the design called Gilmosery, the shape of the building is entirely made by regulations. It derives from the height and the solar exposure and from all the other situations derived from the FAR. [...] In this building, the concept is very straightforward, after having defined the maximum buildable volume. What you see now [contained terrace outside] is not considered buildable volume; in fact, the calculations concerned only the inside. All this space is a plus because it is not included in the built volume. I can create an outdoor space where people have the opportunity to go out without creating a marginal space in connection to the city.

4.3 Group

What's the story of how you get to know this group and how you participated in its activities?

The group was already formed when I joined. After my exhibition in Tokyo in 1989, they called me and invited me to participate. At that time, there were at least 14 members; it was like a study group, and we centered our effort on finding out what we were as Koreans. We discussed the meaning of Modernism, Localism, and Tradition, and the final result was intended as a validation of our culture and identity... We did everything we could. We did not only make several explorations of modern architecture and our legacy, but also organized lectures by architects and artists. We wanted to extend our spectrum of action... In the end, we had an exhibition called "Echoes of an Era" in 1992, and published two books. I believe, in reality, we didn't end up with tangible results. It was more about making a new awareness of the problem of "conservative" society and academia. Now the group broke up, but some members still appear in several events.

What do you think were the falls of the group, why their goals were not achieved?

We could not define our identity. The debate was interrupted and broken apart by individual opinions... but it was very useful for me and my works. Thanks to the group, I understood better what my agenda was and also how to be more persuasive and showcase my works and ideas... The group failed because it didn't define the new Korean Modernism.

This and previous page
Frame
Courtesy of Archium

To have a rich experience of light, it must first be dark. Light is something observed and lived only if there is darkness, and even darkness itself can be perceived only if there is light. If there is only darkness in the universe, we cannot say that darkness exists, because we cannot recognize it. In this way, nothing exists and there is nothing.

Cho Byoung-soo
BCHO Architects

Decadence, Death, and Nature
Paintings, Death, And Skulls
Complete in Its Incompleteness
Function as "Moment of Experience"

Decadence, Death, and Nature

Many of your buildings work with the idea of hypogeum space.

The hypogeum space derives from the negative concept of Yin and Yang in Korean philosophy. Yang is as positive as life; Yin is like the earth: without life. Yang is lively and energetic, but only for a short time and not long enough. Yin is calm and lasts for a much longer time surpassing Yang. Yin is like a mother holding a newborn baby... We are all newborns, and the earth is our mother; It's the same feeling. [...] For example, if I want to use light, I always try to create darkness first. To have a rich experience of light, it must first be dark. Light is something observed and experienced only if there is darkness, and even darkness itself can be perceived only if there is light. If there is only darkness in the universe, we cannot say that darkness exists, because we cannot recognize it. In that way, nothing exists, and there is nothing. All those moments causing contrast help us recognize different entities: light, and darkness, apogee and hypogeum, life and death, male and female. [....]

What was the first time you started analyzing this dichotomy in architecture?

... There were three different moments. The first was when I was little - 4 or 5 years old - my parents took me to their small town in the south. I took a train for 12 hours and then a bus that came only twice a day - spending two days in total. When we arrived, we passed by a beautiful stream, and my mother helped me to walk across, stepping on the rocks. I was fascinated by the water and the reflection on it. I remember touching it... It was one of those lively moments of youth... it was so beautiful! I think architects can feel deep emotions and can appreciate these feelings in the same way as children. The second moment was in elementary school. My school was huge. Imagine that there were 99 students for each class, with only one teacher! It was illegal to have 100 or more students. One day during the lunch break, I heard the dong, producing a deep, slow, and repetitive sound, which meant we had to go back to class. [...] So before I entered the classroom, I felt a kind of attractive smell. A few raindrops began to fall to the ground, releasing the scent of soil in the air... it was so beautiful! When I was 15, the mother of my best friend died - committed suicide... using poison, I remember. I accompanied my friend to bury her in the mountains. There were two or three other people with me and my friend carrying the coffin. At that moment, I noticed that the casket was so heavy. I thought that when people are alive, they are easy to carry around, while when they die, they become extremely heavy. We arrived, and people were standing and waiting. The hole in the ground appeared as a section of clayey soil and roots... There, the sky was so blue, the coffin was so heavy, and the soil section depicted precisely the inside of the ground. They let down the coffin in the ground using a piece of white fabric, making it carefully lie down flat, and covered it with red silk. They then pulled out the white cloth, covered the hole with earth, and then... I didn't know what it was, but for me that moment and space itself were beautiful! [...] Years later, with my nephew, we went for a walk in the hills of Seoul. It started to rain, and I felt the same sensation I felt as a child in the mountain. I think my nephew's generation must experience these lost feelings like water, torrent or rain in the mountains. It's fantastic and beautiful! [...] Then I grew up and, like an atheist without beliefs, I always stopped at the thoughts of many things... These are experiences of my youth, which strongly influenced my professional life as an architect.

Earth House
Photo by Hwang Woo-seop

How did you implement these experiences into architecture?

[...] My first project was my university thesis in 1991. I had studied in Switzerland with professors Mario Campi, Mirko Sardini, and Antonio Ciucci. With them, I had learned about materiality, details, and architectural sensitivity. Then I went back to Korea to develop the thesis. As you can see [showing sketches from the thesis] the project was a simple empty box with some steps going downstairs. It was a house built in compressed earth, taken from the site. It was a project focused on the simplicity of spaces, materials and construction typologies. It insisted on views from the inside towards the sky and the ground. I always tried to incorporate these features into my projects: a hole in the earth; the water on earth; a hole in the hill - where a tree has been uprooted - a hole in the hill covered with tree branches; some wood steps in the earth; steel masses set into the earth; the concrete pavement and steps; and an empty wooden box in the ground. At the Swiss university, I was nominated for the thesis award, but I did not win. They told me the idea was great, but the execution didn't impress. At the time, I didn't yet know how to translate this idea into architecture. Then I took the time, and I thought about who I was and what kind of architecture I was trying to do - yet I'm still looking. I still insist on examining: "How can we create the "moment" of experience without too much effort and using simple shapes?"

Paintings, Death, and Skulls

From where your fascination for simple forms comes?

It's like a simple drink, you know? The taste stays much longer inside you and becomes a much stronger experience. Instead, when you remember complex things, they inevitably become blurred. Simple things create an experience, like rain, water and other essential things like smells. These things remain more imprinted in your mind for a much longer time. For example, I like the works of art dealing with the theme of simplicity, such as Ellsworth Kelly, who creates models and simple geometric shapes... or Donald Judd, a sculptor who always creates autonomous elements and characterizes the space with their simplicity. [...] I too was a painter and made some paintings on experience and perception subjects [Black Ink Skull in Newspaper in 1991]. They explored the way one perceives, experiences, and knows things... All these works were studies I've done to understand how our bodies are sometimes strangely empathetic with specific things and spaces. [...] When you enter a space, how do you perceive it? I did all the paintings in the dark... I had piles of newspapers, and I painted them without looking at them, to investigate what I had in myself. These paintings represent skulls, life, and death... I have a real human skull, and in the past, I always carried one with me even in my car.

Where did you get it?

Through a professor... but it is not very difficult to obtain; there are specialized shops that have recent skulls. But what I had was an older one, found in the mountains within the ground... it is beautiful! [...] My paintings were like adventures made in the dark. I think skulls symbolized well the image of the duality between soft parts of the face, the sharpness of the eyes and nose. For me, painting has been an experimental attempt to represent this dichotomy.

Complete in Its Incompleteness

Your work insists on the issue of the Korean essence of culture and beauty. What are your definitions and personal conclusions?

Earth House
Photo by Hwang Woo-seop

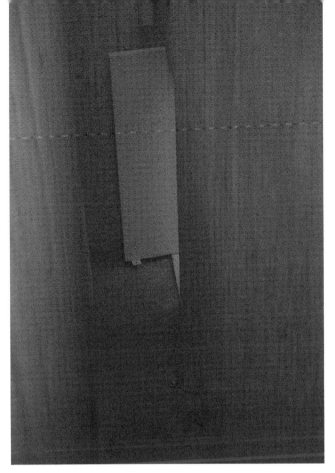

Earth House
Photo by Hwang Woo-seop

Beauty comes from the emptiness, and this is only possible when we are empty. If, however, we have too many desires, we cannot appreciate it. So the real beauty comes from accepting that we are not complete, that we are not perfect. [...] Like our traditional paintings and ceramics, they were not made flawlessly or as intended, but their beauty was intrinsic and generated by that imperfection. It was created from craftsmanship, fire, tools used, and expressive use of ink. All these show actions impressed in the materiality of the object. They are so perfect... It is complete because in its incompleteness it is complete. Our tradition strongly influences Korean architecture and contemporary art, deriving from humble and simplicity. Although the building is simple, its experience is rich. We have created profound experiences using simple materials and showing the process of how they were made. [...] I had taught for two years at the German university [Universitat Kaiserslautern], and in the Design Studio, I was involved in teaching philosophy and contemporary conceptual ideas about architecture in Asia and Korea.

What message would you like to convey to your students?

To better understand it, it is useful to think about the western definition of light that you find, for example, on Wikipedia. Light is defined through Einstein's theories, describing particles, their composition, and how fast they go, etc. But in Eastern culture, light is defined rather as what can only be seen in darkness - where light and darkness unite, balancing each other. [...] Korea, China, and Japan do not have a long history of modern architecture. Not as much as they have on paintings, philosophy, and art... I want to show you a picture [Kim Jung-Hee Wintry Days]. This is 150 years ago; it is so beautiful! The painter was in exile on the Jejo island, in a closed, minute and humble space. The subject he painted was a landscape described in a poem from an ancient Chinese book. If you look closely at the image, you see that there is an essential number of trees, and these are as minimal as space; it's so poetic! [...] When it snows, in a landscape like this, you can see the green much stronger. He painted very carefully; he didn't use much ink, but just strokes of dry ink with a minimum amount of water, emphasizing the feeling of simplicity. The painter writes about the painting: "What do we want more?" ... It is an ambiguous way of life. This philosophy and these ideas were born in China; what we see here is just one of the central root derivations. The painter had cleverly studied Chinese elegance and further developed it by translating it into paintings.

In the same way that feelings can translate from poems into paintings, how can you convert artifacts into architecture?

... Let me show you a picture of a famous ceramic vase [Bowl, Chosun Dynasty 1392-1897]. If you look at the surface, you see that it is not perfect; there are so many irregularities. The Koreans made ceramics very quickly using bamboo sticks, giving the surface a lot of texture... But, if you look at them, the inaccuracy is the real beauty! The vase shows the texture of the material, the way they were made, the speed at which it rotated, and the movements of the craftsman sculpting the clay ... It took just from 10 to 15 seconds to create a jar like this one, which you can read from the surface. [...] Another example is the 'Moon Vase' exhibited at the Leeum Museum here in Seoul. As you can see [showing the image of the architect's monograph], it has an irregular spherical shape. With the technology of the time, they had to do it in two parts, upper half and lower half and then put it together. Only then, it was put together and cooked. Through this action, the parts settled and changed... look at the clear difference between the top

Earth House
Photo by Hwang Woo-scop

and bottom! We can also see how the fire, with its effect, has tilted the form, incorporating its energy into the object. The result will never be perfect; it will always be a bit tilted in different ways. Koreans accept these artifacts as complete and perfect in themselves. In the same period, however, in China and Japan, they forced themselves to make ceramics in a very precise, elegant and "beautiful" way ... For example, some sculptures by Michelangelo were left unfinished. Many people perceived them as incomplete, but now these sculptures are appreciated as finished works. In reality, they are incomplete and imperfect, but... they are beautiful! These are the ingredients, strengths, and values that represent Korean culture, and this could also form a new core for today's architecture. Yes, I'm trying to get right at this point... I would like to understand how would you and other architects use these concepts in relation to the current architectural condition. I don't know if I can answer correctly, but I think I could show these values in some of my projects ... but only thanks to the people who accepted them and my clients who allowed me to build them... But I also think that this thing it's like a rainbow: all the colors are beautiful. You can't choose one in particular, but you can use different ones in different contexts and places. I think this is the same thing with architecture: sometimes you can play with more complex forms, but I don't think it's absolutely necessary to do so ... just like in nature.

In what sense "in nature"?

Nature is imperfect, but in the Eastern philosophy of "imperfection", nature is perfect on its own... we live with it, so we are part of it. For example, if you get up and bathe in the rain, it can't be more perfect than that ... There are different points of view, and it's just about accepting them and living with them. Not everyone accepts these values; someone rejects them and forces me to change what I have designed! [Laughs]

Function as "Moment of Experience"

What can you tell me about the driving factors of the quality of space?

Instead of "quality", I like to call it "moment of experience" placed between different environments - natural and humanmade. For me these moments must sometimes be a shock, sometimes silent, sometimes exciting, and certainly different. This moment can be created through the connection with what is around or sometimes even with dynamics created between themselves.

About function... my work must include the discussion of its foundations and how it affects the creation of architecture ... In the past, "form follows function", now - especially in your work - form follows what?

The form follows emptiness and the earth... In space, you can put any function.

In which way?

For example, here we are in an art gallery [Onground], but this building was built for residential use, and the function is different now.

With the buildings changing constantly, in your opinion, what features should space have to respond to the ever-changing reality?

They may all appear to be small situations, but what comes out of it is powerful.

Earth House
Photo by Hwang Woo-seop

Twin Trees
Photo by Shin Kyung-sub

What happens in these spaces is something that goes beyond the function intended for that specific environment. In two words, it is the experience that exists between the earth and the sky. In this framework, architecture changes, becoming less important... and then becomes nothing. On the other hand, what happens around it is more important. [...] Seasons and natural elements change architecture, leaving traces on materials and structures. As was the case with ancient pottery, the process that has brought this artifact to this day is embedded within the artefact itself. I want to use materials and technologies that lead to this result. So I'm thinking about the building's waterproofing, the roof without the water-catching canal so that it drops straight from the roof wire. Each drop will hit the floor, and in time we can notice a sign stays in the ground and communicates the elements. [...] I aim to take away everything that is not necessary. It is not a minimalist approach, but a real expression of the material and energy imprinted throughout the story and the everyday use of that artifact.

Twin Trees
Photo by Kim Yong-kwan

264

Top left page
Twin Trees
Photo by Kim Yong-kwan

Bottom left page
Twin Trees
Photo by Shin Kyung-sub

Top right page
Twin Trees
Photo by Hwang Woo-seop

Bottom right page
Twin Trees
Photo by Shin Kyung-sub

Essence

YES, you are here among my griefs,
   Like sweet rose leaves in a jar;
Like hallowed things that will lie
Where lovely things have lain,
Yes, you are here,
And here am I,
With things that were, and yet are,
And gathered petals that are dead
And will not live again.

[111]

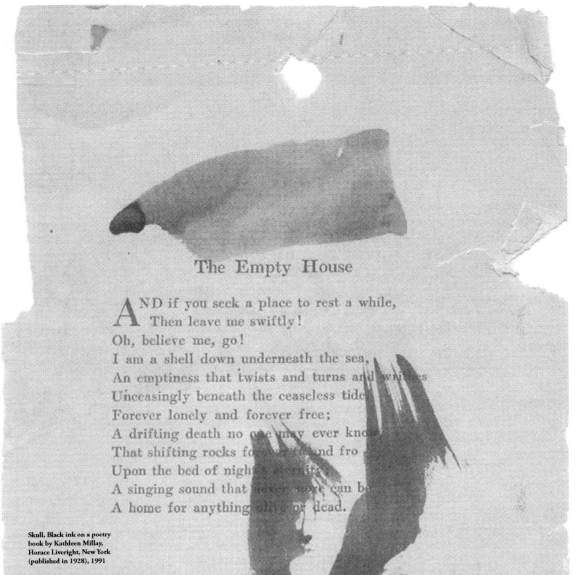

The Empty House

AND if you seek a place to rest a while,
    Then leave me swiftly!
Oh, believe me, go!
I am a shell down underneath the sea,
An emptiness that twists and turns and writhes
Unceasingly beneath the ceaseless tide
Forever lonely and forever free;
A drifting death no one may ever know
That shifting rocks forever to and fro
Upon the bed of night's eternity
A singing sound that never more can be
A home for anything alive or dead.

Skull, Black ink on a poetry book by Kathleen Millay, Horace Liveright, New York (published in 1928), 1991

"Skull" was the work I tried to put those ideas into. I felt the same kind of pulse with my brush strokes on tens and hundreds of pages. These were done on a poem book from 1921 by a unknown poet which I found at a corner of a used bookstore. These book were cheaper to buy than a sketch book with similar paper quality. I felt the time-pass from the autograph of the poet and the original book owner. The book was the site for me to express the skull with Indian ink. The studio residence, which used to be shady house when I purchased at a bargain and converted into my studio space, gives me a pity.

Courtesy of Cho Byoung-soo

[127]

Onground Gallery
Courtesy of Cho Byoung-soo

Onground Gallery
Courtesy of Cho Byoung-soo

Onground Gallery
Courtesy of Cho Byoung-soo

Sometimes, not being able to start from the context, I work with what is missing. When I'm faced by a meaningless context, I look at nearby areas and try to improve the situation. I design a system with the potential to create a positive reaction in the hope of awakening a broader context around.

Kim Min-ji
ISON Architects

Initiatives, Crisis, Building Types
4.3 Group, Returning to Origins
Importing the Context Dilemma
Process Defined by the Context

Kim Min-ji Interview
Photo by the author

Initiatives, Crisis, Building Types

[...] I returned from Italy in 1996 and in 1997 I opened my own studio in Seoul, while there was a heavy economic crisis that lasted a long time... I remember that in those years, I didn't have a real aspiration to understand what architecture really was! [Laughs]. I had to survive, so I tried to make as many projects as possible. Since there wasn't much work, we had to compete with so many other practices, and it was difficult to win some competitions!

How did you find the first clients?

The only way was through acquaintances. Sometimes I did competitions but only as a distraction from the office-work in the studio... I mainly worked on commissions, and I'm still doing so after 20 years.

How has architecture changed since you returned to Korea?

[...] In the '90s the architectural sector was still entirely dominated by residential construction, and the possibilities for small studios like ours - the ateliers - were very limited. The huge residential complexes were highly standardized, and large companies had monopolized the market. This situation had lasted for a long time, from the '80s until a few years ago... In reality, now the market is changing a little. For example, only in the last five years, I started designing homes. Usually, it's the opposite. Young architects start with villas for relatives and then move up to other types of projects. For me, it was the opposite.

Why?

Because of the "baby boom" generation. They were born after the Second World War and lived all their lives in large apartment complexes. Now it's time for them to retire, they are financially wealthy, and many of them want to build their own home. Before it was quite hard to find your place in the market, but in the last five or six years, the situation improved a lot.

4.3 Group, Returning to Origins

[...] At the beginning of the '90s, there was an outbreak of young architects who united under the name 4.3 Group. They gathered to try to change the existing situation and to renew the Korean architectural debate - or to create one. Somehow they succeeded. Now the members of this group are building the most relevant projects... Archium was a member of the group.

How did this group influence you?

[...] 4.3 Group was not that deep or radical in its messages, but they were the only ones who talked about architecture, emphasizing the lack of culture in Korea and giving importance to the idea of returning to a situation of "poverty" of the architecture – in terms of material and shape. After the 1950s, when there were one or two masters [Kim Swoo-geun and Kim Chung-up], there was a long period between the '60s and 70s with no leading figures, and the architectural panorama was left without guidance. Young architects were disoriented, and they just answered to the high demand for large scale residential projects and office buildings. During this confusion, the only attempt to deal with the identity was to put a "traditional roof over a glass box". [...] 4.3 Group started as a reaction to these ideas, and from that, they began looking for alternatives. In the early '90s,

they investigated the traditional architecture, visiting remote areas. They were seeking to find a common thread, the main elements of the legacy that at that time was missing. They organized discussions, analysis, and site visits, spurring a new specific way of doing architecture. Focusing on the origins of Korean beauty in art and artifacts, they came up with in particular the notion of "roughness", which can be seen in everyday objects, natural material, and imperfections.

At that time, were you following the architectural debate?

When it happened, I was in Italy, so for me, it was much more like an echo... Now, I think the movement was a fundamental necessity for the evolution of contemporary Korean architecture. And in one way or another, the process has lasted until now. The old members remained in a state of respect that allowed them to experiment a lot, in total freedom of expression... Their primary purpose was to find the "origins". And whether they've found it or not still remains an open question.

Importing the Context Dilemma

A movement very much in line with Kenneth Frampton and his critical regionalism.

Yes, and likewise, it was an attempt to find a source for a new identity in relation to the context. The discussion on the context was very active, and everyone wondered, "What is the context in Korea?" A concern that touched me personally, and I was determined to learn more... But I couldn't find it! [Laughs]. If you look at Modern Seoul, it is a city with no context. The context is almost impossible to define, study, or fall into any categorization. Here the urban landscape is the result of simple repetitions, which cannot bring you to any theory. For example, in Italy, the context exists, it is not very difficult to find and understand it. All cities have a common and visible urban structure that defines them... Since the birth of Modernity and the adoption of Western typologies, we have had an extreme difficulty in understanding the context and finding strategies on how to deal with it.

[...] It seems that the context is now defined by a very high density dictated by the laws, dealing with solar exposure and standard requirements. This was well presented at the Venice Biennale last year...

Everyone knew that there was a rule that created this context. I think it was fascinating to study how the laws drastically change the space and the architectural and contextual language. [...] Spontaneity can be seen in post-war buildings. You can see that they are different, because even if laws existed in the past, they didn't respect it. Especially in the '60s and '70s, abusiveness was rampant and it made up the context we see today.

A few days ago, I was visiting Gangnam to examine its urban environment. It is mostly based on the circulation of the car and formed by large urban blocks. Inside, however, I found an unexpected situation. Within these mega-lots, there were small-scale architectures and pocket-sized public spaces, with human scale characteristics. Even the most criticized developments can have certain spatial qualities... How would you create new parts of the city where there are no existing structures?

In my practice, I have never thought in these terms... but if I have to, I would like

This and previous page
Red House
Courtesy of ISON Architects

to study the area thoroughly, understand who lives there or lived before, and how its architecture was structured. Even if there is something insignificant and small, I think it is always important to consider it at least, even for a totally new design.

I have worked extensively in China, and very often I happened to work on big projects without any preexisting context or in demolished areas without leaving any trace...

Something similar happened in the '80s. Many parts of the city have been demolished and completely rebuilt. Apartments have been built in which no urban fabric has ever existed... and very "special" things have come out! [Laughs]. All the orientations of the buildings were the same, all with the same height, and painted with the same color.

What would you have done instead?

In my opinion, the most important things are the elements at street level. Speaking of density and quantity, if we had to follow those parameters, we can do it, but what is important is the ground level. We should also look for any kind of inheritance... In the '80s nobody cared. The developers arrived and developed without any sensitivity, using simple hermetic functions, parameters, and numbers... Now, the only thing that distinguishes the buildings are those big number painted on the facade...

Pure and simple alienation.

Yes, the identity of your home is reduced to a number. My mentor, Francesco Venezia, came here once to do a contest and he said: "but... how is it possible that there are these huge numbers and all the buildings are the same?!?". [Laughs]

Process Defined by the Context

Other architects, when they notice that there is no context, make peace with that. But in your work, I can see an almost heroic attempt to work on it.

I think it's due to my training in the studio of Francesco Venezia in Naples and my experience in Italy. When it comes to the architectural context, it is always a decision on how to analyze and understand it, but without limiting ourselves with it. We must start from the assumption that we need to discover its internal logic and consciously decide whether to go in that direction or not: to rediscover a logic or create a new one. The choices are different, but somehow architecture has to do a little bit of everything... and even design buildings similar to what's already there, why not! In my practice, when I design, it is often difficult to connect directly to the context, so I use a little bit of intuition, using what I learned from the Italian school.

Talk me through your design process, but in a situation where the context, in your opinion, does not exist.

Sometimes, not being able to start from what is there, I work with what is missing. When the urban morphology is missing, my process begins with analyzing the missing features - from an intuitive framework that I have in mind. Thinking in a European way, I believe that a proper city should have a solid structure. From this analysis, I can see if this structure is missing. Sometimes there is no vegetation, so I add more greenery than is strictly required.

Marimba House
Courtesy of ISON Architects

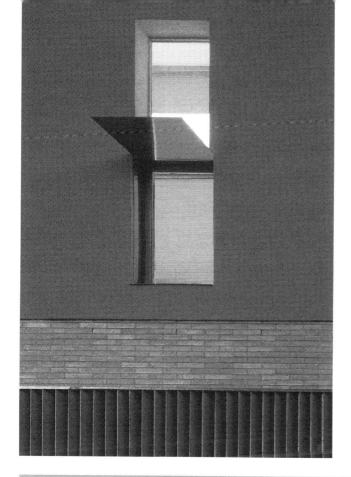

This and next page
Marimba House
Courtesy of ISON Architects

In other situations, you may have empty spaces in a continuous facade created by different buildings, so I try to design a volume to restore this continuity. If there are no squares or public spaces, I also try to integrate this element into the project. [...] when I'm faced by a meaningless context, I look at nearby areas and try to improve the situation. I design a system with the potential to create a positive reaction in the hope of awakening a broader context around.

Historical Sensitivity in a Missing Context

Going on a smaller scale, what logic do you use to define the architectural composition?

We can look at some projects on my website... [...] Yeonhui-Dong House is a project I designed in 2014. The surrounding area was created in the '60s for the middle class, occupying part of an old village. It ended up as a very regular fragmentation because the lots are usually divided into six distinct areas with the house at the back and the garden in front, facing the street. The layout of my project is different... In the plan, the house has the shape of a cross. The cruciform plan does not have symbolic meanings but is all about what it can stimulate around it. By changing the layout and position of the volumes, we were able to create 4 distinct green spaces instead of just one detached from the house and next to the street. In this way, the district would perceive the new space as an integrant part of the community. If we would use this solution over and over, it will be possible to create more integration between the houses, reinstating the ancient structure of the village - what was lost by the modernization... so we could potentially have a positive impact on the entire urban development. [...]

There is a specific will in the choice of materials, colors, and texture... Is the material related to the design choices?

In a way, yes. The houses around had brick walls, so for the new facades, I used copper to have a similar look. The material is not stable and oxidizes over time, producing an effect comparable to exposed bricks... Furthermore, the sloping roof recalls the appearance of the houses of the '60s. I intended to use specific strategies that, over time, will transform the project into an integral part of the village, building complexity, and having the power to influence the surrounding context. This project is not so extreme or radical, but I hope it will have the strength to revolutionize the entire area. [...] In each project, I made an extra effort and tried to achieve this.

There are also several contradictory and complex aspects. Is it a driving concept or just a consequence of your process?

... It is somehow a contradictory logic. On one hand, I want to find a particular dialogue with homogeneity, on the other, I want to break the dynamics of the urban system, even creating something entirely new! For example, in the same village, there were 4 different lots inhabited by 3 generations of the same family. The client wanted to make the house [Marimba House] for his daughter - who was a percussionist - and create other spaces for his family too... I imagined a building plan as an agglomerate: a small village within the village. The entire built space develops around a shared garden. To connect with the houses around, I explored facades made of exposed bricks. I designed a sloping roof and overlapped a cube, generating contrasts with the existing shapes, but connecting

Marimba House
Courtesy of ISON Architects

Iddleul Kindergarten
Courtesy of ISON Architects

it with an orange surface, resembling the brick color. On the other sides, facing the street, I introduced materials similar to the context, instead, for the facades facing the garden, I placed different material such as wood. So, from the outside, one sees all the buildings with regular shapes - respecting the surroundings... Thus, the same building has complete different appearances from the interior and the exterior, creating a contradictory and conflicting logic.

Your architecture has many western characteristics... Does your work have any relationship with tradition?

There is not. I wonder why... Actually, I don't think it's mandatory! [Laughs]. Of course, if I can implement something traditional in my architecture, it might be useful, but still, it's not necessary. I work well even if I don't use traditional concepts; I think it's more relevant and useful to relate to what's around: tangible things of the current time... It is also essential to create a stratification to improve architectural richness. The quality is composed of different layers, deriving from the urban, street, house, green, and human scale... To make layers on top of layers, creating an architecture stratified like an onion! [Laughs].

Iddleul Kindergarten
Courtesy of ISON Architects

I'd like to describe my work as a "Strolling away" architecture. In short, it is an approach that uses traditional tools to solve contemporary requirements such as client, urban code, and site. I use this philosophy to solve all present architectural problems, creating a space as inter-penetration, dynamic with visible and invisible connections.

Kim Hyo-man
Iroje KHM Architects

Indirect Influences
Out from the Game
Form
"Strolling Away"
Future Horizons

Kim Hyo-man Interview
Photo by the author

Indirect Influences

[...] I was very influenced by the SPACE Group. Kim Swoo-geun was the leading exponent and, as you know, he was certainly Korea's most eminent architect. I worked with him when I had my first experience in an architectural firm, and he was a father figure for me and for all of us... when I was still studying, there were also other significant figures for me like Luis Barragan, Frank Ghery and Le Corbusier. These figures have been fundamentals for my education and my work as an architect. From Le Corbusier and Frank Ghery, I learned that architecture has the potential to become a work of art. So from them, I took the idea of analyzing architecture not only as space and function but as a sculptural object with enormous aesthetic possibilities. From Kim Swoo-geun, I certainly have learned the fundamentals and the essential elements of space, learning the true essence of architecture as light and interaction with space... In particular, I analyzed and developed the idea of "folded space" and how the spatial sequence can produce sensations of mystery and surprise, including unconventional spatial dynamics.

Has traditional architecture been a primary or secondary influence for your architecture?

... Do you know the building of the SPACE Group, 1978? This is the most famous and influential modern building here in Korea - which also served as Kim Swoo-geun's studio. Working inside its walls, I absorbed ideas of how tradition can be translated into contemporary architecture... Yes, for this reason, I can say that tradition, and its modern interpretation have strongly influenced my work during my career. [...] Working with Kim Swoo-geun, I was able to extract his knowledge and strategies to modernize the essence of traditional architecture. I took his ideas and tried to develop them even more... But, to answer your question, the tradition was of minor influence on me, I never went looking for the essence of traditional Korean architecture, but somehow I learned it through the teachings of Kim Swoo-geun. [...] Personally, instead of looking for a localized architecture, I try to create a universal one. That's why I collected ideas from the architecture of Kim Swoo-geun and developed them with my view on it, which also reflects the international culture and current achievements in architecture.

Out from the Game

Have the economic boom and the consequent crisis influenced your architecture in any way?

Personally, I was completely out of the dynamics of the economic boom. The financial situation, and the rapid changes of the 80s, did not influence my architecture. [...] I have no nostalgia for that time. I think many damages have been done, but I also think it was somehow inevitable... Now growth has stabilized, and we can do something about it. I believe now is the time, and this is my intention to make the urban context culturally valid. I think it's just an opinion. My architecture has nothing to do with the economic boom and mass production. I was always unique and very different from my colleagues...

The rare privilege of being free.

Yes, I was absolutely free to do my architecture, and in total independence. But my privilege was built by myself, my work... most of my works were a single-detached house, people have seen them, loved them and they asked for me.

How did you manage your earned freedom with strict limits set by the urban planning in Seoul?

The fact of being so regulated does not represent a positive or negative thing ... in the end, it is an excellent tool to rationalize the possibility of the project, especially for clients. When designing in a particular framework, the possibilities are limited, so we are obliged to follow the guidelines. In many cases, my design intentions correspond to the law, so I can rationalize my design and guide the client in a particular direction.

Form

[...] My architecture insists on strong interrelations between "the envelope" and the content. The content is the next step, but it is not separate from the envelope.

Tell me more about the sculptural aspect of your buildings. How do they relate to a specific program?

It is not an easy answer... I think that form and function are connected but at the same time, autonomous. What I do, is to find a form that matches the conditions where the project is located: requirements, codes... everything, you know? I then start and try to solve these problems. The form is only the result of these solutions... I also think that the shape can give you unexpected functions and new potential for spaces besides the obvious. [...] I consider the form and its outcomes a possibility to experiment, rather than choosing a prevalent composition, which can only perform a particular function... My greatest concern is to create a work of art, a beautiful sculpture for people. At the same time, it must be in harmony with the surrounding environment. [...] Experimentation is my goal, not a priori thing, but it is the consequence of what I feel right in that specific situation... When I talk about my projects, I always try to avoid topics like traditional architecture, possible connections or interpretations.

What is your design process?

I come to the final form trying to "reconcile" the three substantial components of architecture: the outer skin, the internal structure and the urban or natural context that surrounds the building ... not counting customer requests and the building code. Finding a balance between these elements, in contrast to each other, I come to create a beautiful image for the building.

What about creating a beautiful sculpture for people. How do you achieve it?

In the same way. The art form is the result of the reconciliation of opposing elements. I think all architectural cases are different, but I admit that I have some recurring features. [...] For example, this project [Purple House] was built on a fairly empty area. There was no building around it. As you can see from the photos, there was only a large mountain. So, in a very intuitive way, I immediately tried to have a mimetic dialogue with these natural elements. [...] In another case, the Archi-Fiore site was adjacent to a sports complex characterized by an iconic concave shape. In this project, I tried to start a dialogue, using resemblance to the building. Only later, I realized that the building was too intense, too dominant to the surrounding context. So, I chose to establish a conversation to find a meeting point. I created a shape in the opposite direction: convex, in contrast to the concave shape of the sports complex. To my surprise, only during the design,

Previous and this page
Ga On Jai
Photo by Kim Jong-oh

I realized that its composition was coming out, somewhat, resembling traditional architecture. In the design process, no element was stronger than others, but all of it found a precise balance. [...] When I design, everything influences me - especially what I see in the area. Sometimes a mountain can play an active role, other times it can be another characteristic building nearby...

"Strolling Away"

[...] I'd like to describe my work as a "Strolling away" architecture. In short, it is an approach that uses traditional tools to solve contemporary requirements such as client, urban code, and site. I use this philosophy to solve all present architectural problems, creating a space as inter-penetration, dynamic with visible and invisible connections. If you look at the urban alleys of Seoul, everywhere, you can see an exciting complexity of space. Urban alleys can be small, swell and exploded over large areas... and suddenly something special comes out. [...] Pretty much, all that I meant about the essence of Korean space, you can still find it in this everyday life. These are the tools I use. [...] Usually, Koreans tend to appreciate the sense of privacy, intimate spaces, and therefore, an introverted architecture, enhancing the feeling of intimacy. For this reason, I often use the courtyard. I think we have to place the concepts of inside and outside at the same level of importance. Japanese architecture, in some ways, is in contrast with this, there is no external space, all they have is interior space, focusing mainly on hidden spaces. Meanwhile, Korea has a strong sense of socialization, and therefore, we want to socialize with our neighbors around us. So we put the equal emphasis on interiors and exteriors. [...] It's a kind of narrative, it's Korean. An intricate labyrinthine space with a certain intrinsic quality could represent this idea... but more than a narrative, it is an archetypal idea of space, which includes path and narration, a sequence of spaces and a walk. When I design, I have a sort of image traced in my mind, from which I learn and cultivate the architectural concept. This architectural space can be the result of all that is connected and where you can have a visual experience.

Future Horizons

Do you think that architecture should push the limits or interpret today's society?

I think my answer should fall on the first hypothesis, because I want to show society a new kind of space. It's not just a matter of adapting and coping with social perception or recognition, but I want to create something unique to push the limit and break the dogmas of architectural space by bringing new experiences...

What new concepts could you use to achieve it?

The very fact of thinking of "new concepts" it's a very Western concept... I intend to go beyond the long-term colonization of culture by the West.

How to get beyond the Western ideas?

In a sense, I would like to change the dynamics that have always existed between Western and Eastern architecture. [...] The "Korean Brand Scape" is obvious now. We can describe it as technologically advanced but not culturally sophisticated... I think there's a big difference. So I believe Samsung isn't like Steve Jobs. It is not creative and cannot produce what the MAC is doing in the United States and in the world. [...]

Island House
Photo by Kim Jong-oh

What do you think is the Korean dream?

I don't know anything about Korean dreams, and I can't care less.

What is the city of your dreams compared to what you see in Seoul?

At the moment there is an extreme situation, we have no public spaces - or they are insignificant. So my dream would be to find a way, together, to maximize public spaces and create a system, allowing the city of Seoul to enhance the small public that we have and do more with them... But the context structure is very chaotic, and there is no harmony. Seoul has gone through moments of serious building speculation: there is no cultural context. Until a few years ago, there was no way of thinking about it. We have an urban structure that is currently missing, vanishing the culture and identity of the city of Seoul. [...] Seoul developed in a tumultuous period, many things could not be taken into account. Those were fast times, we were running!

What is your personal formula to solve the problem?

I think it's a political question and the government must address this problem. I believe the solution will be found over time. It's such a complicated process, with so many problems to deal with that it is not possible to find a solution for everything immediately. I am convinced that within this process, architects like myself and others can give their efforts to improve the situation ... The most important thing is "scale", a particular human scale that creates a distinct atmosphere, closely related to the quality of the space. In many areas of Seoul you can find these features, especially in traditional areas, and sometimes even in some contemporary developments. I think it's due mainly to the interface we use between architecture and public space, an interface very similar to the integration between internal and external areas, in which the narrow streets have almost become a projection of the interior spaces.

Island House
Photo by Kim Jong-oh

This and next page
Kyeong Dok Jai
Photo by Kim Jong-oh

This and next page
Purple Hill House
Photo by Kim Jong-oh

When I returned to Korea, people asked me: "You studied abroad. Can you convert tradition into modernity? "But it's a conversation I've never found interesting. Tradition is part of me, and somehow it comes out, but I don't try to do it... So, if you want to translate the Hanok into modern architecture, just forget about it!

Kim Jun-sung
Architecture Studio hANd

Factories Like Museums
Training Abroad
Crisis and Economy Influence Architecture
A Place, Not an Architecture

Kim Jun-sung Interview
Photo by the author

Factories as Museums

[...] I would like to show you some photos of a project in Paju Book City. Now it is under construction and will be completed soon. [...] In the building, there are three different functions, office, production area, and an exhibition. One of the crucial elements is the landscape, structuring the workshop through gardens...

It looks almost like a museum.

[Laughs], it's actually a Ping Pong equipment factory!

How did the client agree on such a design for industrial construction?

We presented the first idea and doubted ourselves a lot. The costs would have been higher, but he was enthusiastic. So we ended up building it as the render.

Training Abroad

I studied only one year here in Korea. Usually, in the first year, you learn nothing about architecture but only a general study of many disciplines. The following year, for the bachelor's, I changed university, and I followed my parents when they emigrated to Brazil. So I received the first real architectural lessons at the Mackenzie University of São Paulo.

Why did you emigrate?

For different reasons. In Korea, there were problems of political stability, but also it was compelling to have a chance to go abroad. At that time, the dream for Koreans was to emigrate, and most of the families who had the opportunity did so. Brazil doesn't seem a common destination like USA, Australia, Canada or Europe. [...] I guess it was more for my father, he often traveled for work, and he visited different countries. After visiting Brazil, he got impressed by the low racial discrimination, unlike the United States and other nations where integration, in his opinion, was more difficult. So there was a higher possibility to restart in Brazil.

How was the situation? It was a tumultuous chapter for South America.

Chile was just after the *coup d'état*, and it was tough, but Brazil was not like that. It was 1976, at the end of the military government, and from the economic aspect, it was fine. I stayed there until 1982, the time to finish my studies, and then I moved to New York at Pratt Institute, and I completed my studies there.

Why did you move to New York?

I wanted a more conventional teaching system. I remember in Brazil, we put nothing on paper for the first two years! Education was focused on discussions. There were all sorts of groups about the role of an architect and the profession. The conversations were from a social, artistic, and cultural understanding, all of which went around architecture but did not get to the point. I thought about it and decided that that situation did not suit me, and I looked for a university with a complete educational program. The USA was right for me... I had studied for two years in New York, and I received excellent professional training. After that, I worked full time in the architectural office of one of my teachers for almost five years, a company called Mayers & Schiff Architects. John Schiff and Robert Mayers were professors at the Cooper Union and Pratt Institute.

What was the job like?

The firm was small, but it was interesting because there were many intellectuals, John Schiff was an artist, and the discussion was always stimulating. With the involvement in the office, I was exposed to many ideas and information... But the question of "what is my point of view on architecture?" was growing significantly inside me. I decided to study more to find "my way", and I went to attend Columbia University. [...] Thanks to a school program, I worked in Alvaro Siza's studio in Portugal... In retrospect, I guess this experience, instead of transmitting technical knowledge of architecture, I understood much more how to be an "Architect" rather than how to practice architecture. In New York, I was an energetic, almost aggressive student. When I spoke with Siza for the first time, I wanted to impress him. So I made a speech that seemed like propaganda about how I love architecture. When it ended, Siza looked at me with an inquisitive stare and said: "I do not love architecture, I love myself!" [Laughs]. This and other experiences made me question everything, both my design purpose and what it means to be an architect. Only later, I fully understood his sentence, how he intended the activity of being an "Architect". It was not an activity he wanted to do, but it was a way of living life. And this point is one of the main things I received from him. I learned to be reflective and not to be afraid to wait, both for defining my architectural principles, also to feel complete and realized as an architect and a person.

Then in 1992, you founded your own studio in Korea. What made you come back?

My decision to return to Korea was not a priori decision. I came here for an exhibition in 1991, and as soon as I arrived, I was covered by offers from clients who wanted me to build. People blocked me and begged me: "please design my house!" [Laughs] In the early '90s in Korea, the economy was exploding. It was the time when enormous quantities were built with no quality. I was in my 30s, and I was given a chance to be in a privileged condition. I decided at first to stay for a project or two. In short, the period became two years, then I waited another two years and so on. And now I am still here! It was an excellent opportunity for me, and I hardly notice the time passing. [Laughs] When I arrived, architectural education in Korea did not exist yet. Imagine, I was immediately invited to be a professor and to create the first master's course here in Korea. All the institution programs were engineering, so we founded the first architecture school, Konkuk University, and I was its first dean. Now the situation has changed substantially, the importance given to architecture today differs totally from the '90s. Architecture was considered engineering back then, so even if we designed a particular staircase that could be used as furniture, the client did not want it because he considered it as a decoration, and something he should take care of, not the architect.

A revolution has taken place in the culture of clients...

Yes, there was no interior design culture. They said: "you are the architect and then you design the structure and the facade but inside I'll take care of it!". The interior was their world, so we could not touch it. In several occasions, I designed parts of the interior, but everything was trashed. Now the culture is different, and many clients ask me to design even an interior. As well the university has changed and now is very similar to what you can find overseas. Many professors studied abroad, came back, and carried out what they have learned. Now I would not recommend

Mimesis Museum
Photo by Jeffry Sandy

Mimesis Museum
Photo by Jeffry Sandy

learning elsewhere. To study here is enough... But you should always go abroad to gain experience. At the beginning of the '90s, I expected this kind of shift in education to take off, maybe, in fifty years, but it happened so quickly!

Crisis And Economy Influence Architecture

In Korea, we still have a unique situation.... Let's say I design a building, and I have been awarded by the Korean Architectural Association. If in the next year this construction doesn't produce any monetary value or interest, the building is doomed, and it will be for sure demolished. The cost of the land is so high that you must profit... So we have to deal with a situation in which all other aspects are in the background. [...]

There was a significant change in architectural practice after 2008.

Before the crisis, the main expectation of the owner was how to get more square feet built. But the clients' culture has progressed, and now they want to have something more than just make the maximum volume. That's why they are currently looking for creative design solutions.

What are the clients looking for?

... Something unusual that they have not seen before or that can attract people and clients with. In recent years it has evolved, and now they want more mature architecture. They want to appreciate the actual quality of construction, details, and space. We are moving in the right direction.

Has the crisis improved the level of architecture?

[...]If the project of the Ping Pong factory had been planned before the crisis, it would never turn out to be like that. After the change, they wanted to build something special or creating an innovative environment for the people who work inside that factory. [...] After the crisis, the clients want to be at the forefront of the business field, which I consider a significant and positive change. The solution for them now is to focus on the quality of architecture. [...]

Seems like a critical point in history when Korea took a break, re-booted and restarted...

... and we are still inside this phenomenon. The factory was a project with a reduced budget, and we were quite surprised because they pushed the features that made it over-budgeted. For example, the height of the floors was one and a half that of the building aside, increasing the costs compared to the volume. The client insisted on doing it anyway because he had already understood the possibilities. With higher architectural quality, he could quickly lease spaces which could justify the increase in construction costs. Nowadays people do not just want roomy or well-established spaces, they want something new and better.

A new renaissance for Korea?

For the quality, it's a renaissance, but from quantity perspective, it's still a recession!

A Place, Not an Architecture

Mimesis Museum
Photo by Jeffry Sandy

[...] When a client enters my studio, I always start by saying "I do not want to

Mimesis Museum
Photo by Jeffry Sandy

make an architecture to be remembered by a form, but I want people to remember it by the place and what it can create".

How would you achieve it?

By making people feel differently, influencing their sense of space. For example, when people come into my office, they sit where you are sitting now [in front of a large window facing a small garden]. I do not make them recall this experience by the curved shape of this court behind us. Instead, I want everyone to recognize the beauty of this lovely garden in front of you... Do you agree? So the intention shifts from the image to the experience and well-being. It seems to me essential to reflect on how space and people can be connected through experience. [...] I was born and raised in a *Hanok*. I have a strong memory of the courtyard of my house and the view of the mountains outside the window... When I was sitting on the living room floor, sometimes, from there, you could see the mountains beyond the fence. I lived there for 19 years before leaving Korea. I have several special memories of the traditional spaces, so I do not mind a structure of the house with a big void... it's ample space, but it's not just empty: it's intentionally empty. I presume flexibility as the main feature.

Is it more about architectural possibilities or functional spaces?

Both functional and structural. The structure can be changed. Many parts bend and move and can be divided into several spaces. It can be subdivided into different spaces, or it can be completely unique. Sometimes when I look at these spaces, I stop and think "what is the meaning of this function? What is it based on? *Hanok* has physical flexibility because it can be subdivided into many spaces. But it also has the capability to bring you into contact with nature. The courtyard can sometimes become an interior as well as an exterior. These are all the characteristics that people who lived in a traditional architecture expect to have inside, and we can have them available for design. Architectural identity is a long and complex discourse, and I try to stay away from it.

What is your private agenda?

My question is, "how can I create an architecture which follows the international standards?". But to do so, I have to do it with my taste and my beliefs. When I returned to Korea 20 years ago, the main issue was to understand what Korean architecture was. And people asked me, "You studied abroad. Are you able to convert tradition into modernity?" But it is a conversation that I never found interesting. It's not that I don't want to put effort into it, but this discourse cannot be solved with statements and experimentations. This matter can only be cleared up with maturity through time. It shouldn't be translated quickly! If architecture is beautiful, it is not important how you call it, European, Asian, or Korean. When you do it, there is always a certain problem lurking. If we study traditional architecture, it is fantastic, and the memory is still inside of us. And it is already enough... If I have to be honest, perhaps unconsciously this happens sometimes. [...] Tradition is part of me and somehow comes out, but I do not try to do it... So if you want to translate the Hanok into modern architecture, just forget about it!

Mimesis Art House
Photo by Jua Chae

Mimesis Art House
Photo by Jua Chae

This and next page
Mimesis Art House
Photo by Jua Chae

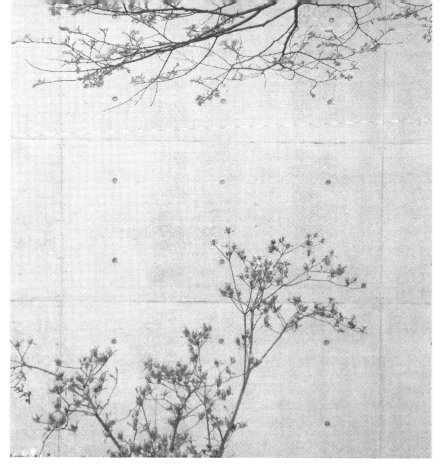

To speak of "public space" would seem a cliché... Unfortunately, it has to do with the abuse of the word "public". Architects use it just like a slogan, but in reality, they do not create anything public. It is true hypocrisy! They only make residual spaces with a "green" label on it. It is essential to designing public spaces as an integral part of architecture.

Choi Moon-gyu
GaA Architects

Choi Moon-gyu Interview
Photo by the author

Ssamziegil: The Disruptive Effects of Public Space

[...] Have you already visited Ssamziegil in Gwanhun-dong? It is not far from where you are staying.

Yes. It is for sure a remarkable building with explosive potential...

Now the environment is a bit changed, it has become very dirty, and there are graffitis everywhere - so many people visit it every day! Both the client and several consecutive owners have had a lot of problems... The project focused on the public quality and was designed as an attraction to appeal to people's attention. But this was so effective that now it had become a kind of issue. To contain the flow of people, the owner had decided even to charge an admission fee! But the people started asking, "Why should we pay to take just a picture?". The owner - even though he was full of his rights to do so - made people feel a sense of injustice. The visitors treated the building as it was not merely commercial but rather public and as an integrated part of the public urban environment. I remember after these issues, there were attacks on the owner's website. That is why the landlord had to give up his battle and abandon it... Since the opening, this had happened twice, and a few other owners had taken over after him. [...]

Everything emerged from the composition of the building...

Yes, and somehow it was all my fault! [Laughs]. All these problems, both degradation and overcrowding were a chain reaction, leading to a difficult situation. Moreover, the price of land in the area has increased remarkably due to the proximity to this building. [...] This building was a structure, so public that was it able to define a new archetype with shocking impacts at the urban level.

And now, the Seoulians are the de facto owners.

Yes, in a softer way, I try to achieve it in all my projects. I want to raise public accessibility to buildings... I entirely avoid any formal aspects, and I focus primarily on connectivity and accessibility. In Ssamziegil, the pedestrians are pushed to look inside, and the ones inside have many opportunities to find interesting and instagrammable views. [...] The strong sense of connection links the building to the urban fabric both visually and physically.

City Interface

You often use the concept of "in-between space", an area half-way between the building and the urban context, leaving people to interact and to increase a dynamic pedestrian flow.

... Maybe it is trivial reasoning, but when I was a kid, there were no cars in the street. The road was for us children, and we could use it to play. When I was a teenager, the vehicles had already occupied all the space. From that moment until now, all the empty spaces have been dominated by cars, and at the same time, no effective additional policies has been introduced to create more public areas. I miss a lot this kind of "space-appropriation". Nowadays, I think it is a big problem, causing severe cases of depression. I often think about the role of the buildings within the city framework, and I am opting more and more to "open structures" which promote public spaces - even where is not possible to do so or where urban planning rules do not endorse it. If you think about it, it

is a way to leave a good legacy for the generations to come. [...] I know: hearing myself speaking about "public space" would sound like a cliché... It is a pity, and I think, unfortunately, it has to do with the overuse of the word "public". Architects, from all over the world, are using it just as a brand. They support projects with this slogan, but in reality, if you go deeper, they don't create anything public. It is real hypocrisy! What they do is just residual space where to put a "green" label on it. Instead, it is essential to design public spaces as an integral part of the architecture, or better, as an extension of it.

Innovative Images vs Innovative Spaces

You had created a proposal for the area where the 'Dongdaemun Design Plaza' now stands. What do you think of the project realized by Zaha Hadid?

[...] The commission had invited many architects, both international and local ones. Although I had just opened my studio, I had the opportunity to participate and to compete with international caliber architects - the project had enormous potential for impacting the city. My design idea was very different from the DDP you see now. The current structure has a single main entrance coming throughout the metro, all other doors are not very accessible from the street level - yes, inside there is a relatively fluid environment, but it feels almost like being trapped. When you are inside, the main level is underground, and you cannot see anything outside - you don't feel being part of the city. It is undoubtedly a unique space, but it lacks integration, and it behaves as a closed and self-standing object... I think Zaha has built a self-referential legacy. I condemn this attitude used all over the world. [...] The DDP has replaced an area with an essential trace of the past, starting back in 1925 with the first stadium built in Korea - the Dongdaemun stadium, and the baseball stadium Gocheok-Dong. My project instead was based on the preservation of the green sports fields. If you can imagine, this would have been able to entirely shift the attention from the built volumes to the empty and green spaces. The rest of my proposal evolved on the distribution of many separate and small elements connected through many pedestrian connections - avoiding the isolation of megastructures and improving the legacy and integration between the city and the project.

The beginning of the DDP project was a significant date as well for a substantial cultural shift in Korea. 2008 marked the changing in the minds of the clients - from "square meters' logic" to "excellence logic". So for many other local architects, this meant more projects and more quality in architecture. What is your experience?

The recent economic crisis has not very much influenced me. I think because my work is very varied since I have both public and private clients, large and small projects. This brings me out of all the logic connected to the "FAR game" [Floor Area Ratio, the title of the Korean Pavilion at Venice Biennale 2016]. I am inclined more to multiple directions. I believe one of the main reasons is because more than 50% of my projects come from competitions. They vary in types from schools, offices, to residential buildings at all the possible different scales.

You enjoy the possibilities of competitions?

[Laughs] I do not think it's that amazing to deal with competition, because

Ssamziegil
Photos by Kim Yong-kwan

Ssamziegil
Photos by Kim Yong-kwan

Arumdri Media
Photos by Kim Yong-kwan

there is so much work involved and only few possibilities to win. But to have such a broad and different range of built designs, it was - as it is now - a winning strategy for my practice.

In a complex and fragmented situation like here in Seoul, large-scale design projects are very challenging.

[...] I have done several large-scale urban projects and new districts plan, and it was always challenging to make them effective. I wanted to escape the typical logic based on rigid grids, creating a much more fluid city - do not interpret it from the organic sense of the term - to develop systems to fight the alienation and wasted and disconnected space. We need to find a logic that can create a superimposition of different functions to support and to develop exciting urban life and stimulating the sense of belonging. On many occasions, when the commissions examine my projects, they say, "this project could be brilliant, but it has nothing to do with Urban Planning". [...] Now the situation is slightly getting better, but they are still not that used to these types of projects yet. They are people connected to the government, fairly conservative, who in the early 80s used to work with large technical real estate companies.

Podium as a Realized Utopia

In many projects, you create plazas on top of accessible communal podiums. This space has public properties that are impossible to confine...

Sometimes it derives from laws that allow open space to be less burdensome on FAR, such as terraces and balconies. Some other times it is a wish of the client to have more open spaces, but in me, it always prevails a willingness to have aggregative and open design choices to localize different functions. [...] I want to create altered sensations in different parts, attracting interest and surprise. I use different materials, building separate envelopes, emphasizing the complexity of the aggregation. So, the spatial experience takes place sometimes in a wooden, concrete, or a glass "box". Each material gives different impressions, and specific elements are more up for one or the other function. I also create small spaces with some privacy features to provide the possibility - why not - to smoke a cigarette on the roof. I want to create different functional pockets with unique opportunities. [...] In the project 'The Student Union' I design almost all the spaces underground, this makes the roof very accessible to the public. It is actually a massive building but with a low impact as it is hidden in the ground. It joins many pedestrian connections and different levels, intersecting and making the area porous. It all stems from a profound analysis of the urban and sociological situation. The loop above the building is designed to both see soccer matches and as a "stage" over the city. When the structure is closed, you can still always access its spaces - distributed in open and closed parts at first, second, and third level. I am a firm believer in the mixture of different levels and spatial fluidity inside - and on the outside as well - to mix programs within the architectural complex... I think this is a purely Asian complexity, partly shaped by tradition but also by current city dynamics.

It has always been considered quite utopian to create a separation between pedestrian and car fluxes. How does this logic work in your projects and why it has not failed - like in many all-encompassing structures from the past?

I think everything is explained in its complexity. In the 'Centennial Memorial Hall' [University of Seoul] there are more than 25 doors to access the building -

somehow for the caretakers and cleaners, it is a real nightmare. [Laughs] I know
- it is a little crazy because usually in buildings there is only the front and back
door... The important thing is that a person can get anywhere and move anywhere.
There are also spaces that are half-way between the exterior and interior. Having
some precautions and protections, these can be used both under the sunshine
and the rain. My generation has learned these things from school, but they have
not done enough. In reality, my colleagues' way of doing is more about creating
a brand to differentiate themselves from all the others. This way doesn't come to
terms with the condition that we have here. [...]

Critical Moments of the Career

[...] I studied at Colombia University, then I went to Japan for a year to work
for Toyo Ito. Back in Korea, I have worked in medium-sized studios for nine
years. Later, I founded my office, and I became a professor.

**In your buildings, I see something from Steven Holl, from Toyo Ito, and
related to American architecture... I also see some experimentations derived
from research and something with Critical regionalism features. It seems
that you try to escape from a defined language and style...**

After the US, I went to Japan because I felt I could not do anything in Korea...
I felt the oppression of technical architecture that did not leave the possibility
to express the new ideas I had learned abroad. In Japan, there was an active
discussion about space and social dynamics focused on changes in society:
Nomadism, urban flows of people, movement and the shift in family structure,
but they avoided any reference to formal gesture altogether - it was challenging,
I do not lie, I had to learn both Japanese and improve my English... Since
then, everything has changed so much, and meetings with foreign colleagues
have become a daily occurrence. But I think the most formative experience
was in 'Paju Book City' project - a real collective effort. There were so many
good architects! Every time I visited the site I saw new projects, I discussed
with the architects and I was always learning something new - this defined a
lot what my position and my architectural thinking are now. Thanks to this
experience, I have analyzed my production of previous years with different eyes
and understood much more of what I have done and what I want to do in the
future.

Only Villa Savoye Can Remain the Same

How to build a "positive" urban fabric? What do you teach your students?

It is a political matter. The prices of apartments continue to rise, and people
are pushed to go out, but far away from the center, there are fewer services
and lower quality of life. They can also choose to stay in the city, but have to
settle for very tiny spaces. We have to create solutions for these people. Usually,
the quality of the apartment is the most appreciated and standardized by the
market economy. So it is something that I can hardly change. On the other
hand, public space is much more flexible for good design. It is an element that
I can work on, and that can make a substantial impact at the qualitative level
- apartments are a lost battle, and you have to forget it for a moment to focus
on the interface between the condo and the parking, between the parking and
the road and the road and the city. I do not want to throw away my time in
designing luxury or duplex apartments, because these are already quite fixed

This and next page
W Houses
Photos by Kim Yong-kwan

진리
Verita

학생회관

This and next page
SSU Student Union
Photos by Sun Nam-goong

and dictated by the market. 'Ssamziegil' was surprising. People used it very differently from how I designed it. For example, I had intended the spaces to increase the movement but instead were used as spaces to stay... We cannot know everything. [...] As well as for the grand buildings of the past, we must allow people to renew them for contemporary uses. Structures must serve more than 30 or 40 years, so we need to understand this situation to make architecture that makes sense. Architecture is not like a work of art on display at the museum, but it is something that has to be used and therefore changed. Apart from 'Villa Savoye', which evidently must be preserved as it is, most of the architecture is not like that. It is the natural cycle of life.

Previous, this, and next page
SSU Student Union
Photos by Sun Nam-goong

This and previous page
Y Study House
Photos by Sun Nam-goong

This and next page
H Music Library
Photos by San Nam-goong

This and next page
UOS Centennial Memorial Hall
Photos by Sun Nam-goong

This and next page
UOS Centennial Memorial Hall
Photos by Sun Nam-goong

Do you know how Koreans drink liquor? They use two hands, supporting one hand with the other. It represents a ceremony, an attitude of elegance... for me the gesture is culture... The doors I design are tall, heavy, and with a thin handle. The speed of the movements and the dynamics of the gestures change you.

Choi Wook,
ONE O ONE Architects

Culture of Gesture
Discontinuity, Find the Missing Link
Concept vs Sensation
Elements of Architecture
Philosophy in Architecture, Details and Prototype
Not a Facade
Quality of the Space

Choi Wook, Interview
Photo by the author

Culture of Gesture

Do you know how the Koreans drink liqueur?

No, please explain it to me.

They use two hands, supporting one hand with the other. [...] This ceremony represents an attitude of elegance and courtesy... for me the gesture is culture. For example, a door: if we design a conventional one - therefore a light door - it can be opened very easily, even with two fingers. The speed of movements and dynamics of gestures do not change from the interaction with the object... it does not affect you. Space, in this way, becomes neutral. If we look at the doors I use in my projects, we see they are tall, very heavy and, on the opposite side, they have a very thin handle. Here, the door forces you to use two hands to open. You push, and slowly the door opens. If you arrive with a certain speed, you touch the object, and this inevitably transforms your dynamic, leading you to encounter the space in another way, transforming your state of mind, and the experience of the architectural space itself... Do you understand me? I am a strong supporter of space that can influence you, and take you somewhere else. [...] I do not design spaces but actions that affect people's feelings and lives... I remember a client once told me: "your architecture doesn't have a Korean language and does not appear to be Korean but somehow gives me absolutely a Korean sensation".

Discontinuity, Find the Missing Link

How would you evaluate the cultural and architectural situation in the city of Seoul?

If you look at the city, it is clear that we are in a severe cultural crisis. If we think of centuries ago, Korea has always had a well-structured Confucian culture. Art, literature, and architecture were at the highest levels. In the last two centuries, due to wars and invasions, it has gone through periods of growth and destruction, reducing critically. [...] It was 300 years ago when the Japanese invaded and left both the nation and the culture in ruins. Many intellectuals had remained repressed in both economic and cultural poverty... To return to a high cultural level, it took us more than 100 years. [...] More recently, with the wars of the last 70 years, the Second World War and after the conflict between the North and the South, we have lost the hardly reacquired specific aspects of our culture. You know, history always repeats itself... My biggest concern as a person of culture is to revitalize Korean architecture as it has been in the past.

How would you reconnect the current situation in Korea with its culture?

For me, the point to connect to is right before the destruction, colonization, and invasion. [...] I want to reestablish the lost culture. In some ways, I imagine a parallel society where these events didn't destroy it - do not misunderstand me, at the same time, I also want to create an architecture closely linked to the contemporary condition. Imagine if our history continued in a fluid and evolving way, what would Korea look like now?

Creating a disconnected utopian reality but at the same time connected with the contemporary situation. A very ambitious mission... How do you plan to succeed?

It is a very delicate matter... [...] the intent is not to deny the Japanese experience or

H Residence
Courtesy of
ONE O ONE Architects

the American influence, but at the same time, I want to bring out the Korean essence, accepting what is there today without trying to ignore the traces of the past. [...]

Concept vs Sensation

I started working in Korea only after studying in Italy.

It often happens that when one is abroad, one can look at his own culture with different eyes.

Yes, but I think it especially happens if you study in countries like Italy, where you are forced, somehow, to go deep into culture... In my Italian experience, I was amazed by how much the education was focused on tradition - and the analysis of so much historical architecture. It made me reflect on myself and Korea, realizing that I did not know much about my own culture! So, when I returned to Korea, I picked up the history, and I researched it in depth for a long time.

What was the most memorable time abroad?

At the university, I was impressed by the Platonic conception of the project - in the sense of insisting on a "precise" concept. Looking at history, in Korean and Asian architecture, the concept never existed. Unlike the West, the concept is of secondary importance to the balance between the world and nature around us: architecture is like water and therefore fluid... At the University of Venice, I remember once a professor gave me the task of analyzing a project by Le Corbusier's - Villa La Roche - with only drawings and photographs from books. The other students had talked for more than half an hour... but for me it was impossible. So I told the professor: "I cannot talk about something I have never seen or experienced, I need direct experience, I have to go to Paris!" He replied, "No, you do not have to go, you have to analyze through reasoning". At that time, it was a totally foreign approach to me. From this, I understood the way of designing of Western architecture, and I reformulate my principles of architectural design to adapt to the western ideas... Upon returning to Korea, the circumstances were different, and I realized that I had to reformulate my architectural principles once again.

Elements of Architecture

[...] In Italy, I had the basis to face an in-depth historical reading, and when I returned home, I studied Korean literature...

What are the key aspects you discovered?

They are different and derive from the *Hanok*. [...] The first is the variation in section of the podium due to the heating technology called *Ondol*. The hot vapors from the kitchen spread below the floor to reach the rooms positioned above. [...] The kitchen and the rooms had to be at the same level or higher, so the traditional structure always went up and down - Frank Lloyd Wright was so impressed by the *Ondol* that he invented the radiant floor heating, introducing it in the United States. Unlike China or Japan, where the podium is more straightforward or even flat, in Korea, there is a tradition of these height variations... and something that can be implemented in contemporary architecture. [...] The second, which is common to all Asian architecture, is a layout that alternates full - rooms - and voids - gardens - in a repetitive pattern. This derives from the philosophical

H Residence
Courtesy of
ONE O ONE Architects

H Residence
Courtesy of
ONE O ONE Architects

H Residence
Courtesy of
ONE O ONE Architects

concepts: human power doesn't surpass that one of nature. [...] We must foresee a balance... The most important thing is to understand how nature and the environment around works. Once done, it is possible to create architecture, but the form of architecture is secondary. In practice, this translates into a shifting of importance from architecture to emptiness. [...] The third component is the duality between lightness and heaviness. In traditional architecture, we see a very "heavy" podium and very light vertical elements made of paper or wood. In my architecture, I use this contrast between heavy and light materials. [...] The fourth is certainly bringing nature inside, using light. For example, when we see a shadow of a plant on a white wall, nature will integrate to the interior space, bringing life inside the architecture. [...] The fifth is the materials which reveal an idea of simplicity like the polished stone floors, reflecting the architectural elements that surround it. [...]

Philosophy in Architecture, Details and Prototype

Returning to the relationship between the floor and the wall, I think it is interesting what you achieve when these two elements meet. What is the principle you use to define the tectonics?

If we look at the various elements we encounter in the buildings, we observe a lot of glass, metal, and stone. These are obviously different materials, but from my personal point of view, they are very similar. They are all materials derive from stone. For this reason, I am convinced that these materials have no distinction but behave similarly, especially in the way in which they meet one another. So my job is to make them "meet" in a very simple way. Our focal point is the reaction produced by these elements at these specific points. For this reason, I would like to stress that details do not represent the form but how these two elements meet. [...]

Not a Facade

[...] Everything relates to a system that cannot be described or even photographed! In our architecture, photographic presentation does not give credit to the real space. The image, thus generated, is not able to represent spatial qualities... See this very famous painting from the Renaissance period that depicts the imperial palace in Seoul while in the West, in the same period, perspective was a very determining factor in arts. If we look at Korea, the perspective is not essential; instead, the structure is based only on the relationship between the spaces...The West perceives reason while the East senses the feelings. [...] Do take note that so far, I have not spoken in any way of architectural form or composition. In fact, I think it's not relevant. What we try to do in our studio is to go beyond the fashionable "strong image". For example, I do not want to focus on the facade of a building... If we look at the traditional Korean architecture, we see that the facade is absent. As a result for me, the facade is a secondary issue.

I think this is evident in your HC office project, especially in the facade treatment...

Yes, there, the facade is absent. You see? Details are indispensable for the architectural language. It is all about the interaction between detail and nature and how this changes through the changing of light and seasons. [...] The whole facade is created by overlapping elements... I like to say that this facade does not exist because it changes continuously. If we look at a close up picture of the details, we realize that it cannot be represented.

Quality of the Space

In your architecture, there is always the tendency to rather create a character of the space through visual links... You intend a certain quality, not through physical complexity but toward a more profound perception... The person who visits this space is as if he had an augmented experience.

Yes. If we look at traditional paintings, it is actually like that, there is not only one point of view, but the overall image is a representation of impressions. Exactly like in the cinema, in which the combination of the long shot, medium shot and close-up determine the depth of the image and give the right composition of the photograph. So, the action creates space. If we look at the transparency of the materials used, we see how this affects the perception of the dynamics of the space. In other words, we do not accomplish "space"... but space enters in action. My goal is to transform a plain space with a mono perspective in a multi-perspective one - as in oriental art or painting. In Eastern art, there are always three different perspectives, because you do not just want to look at the landscape, but because you want to feel it.

This and next page
HC Office Building
Courtesy of
ONE O ONE Architects

This and next page
HC Office Building
Courtesy of
ONE O ONE Architects

I like to describe my approach to architecture with the word kindness... My way is not focused on showing greatness or extreme forms; I do not like that. When I design a building in a particular context, I always try to show that specific architecture is new, but at the same time, it could give the feeling of something always existed there.

Kim Jong-Kyu
M.A.R.U. network

Human Scale
Crisis, Creativity, and Heritage
Context and Project

Kim Jong-Kyu Interview
Photo by the author

Human Scale

[...] I like to describe my approach to architecture with the word kindness... My way is not focused on showing greatness or extreme forms; I do not like that. When I design a building in a particular context, I always try to show that specific architecture is new, but at the same time, it could give the feeling of something always existing there... So, my approach is not a decorative, extravagant, or fantastic one... not even a proper way "following" the context, nor creating a balance with it... it is more about creating an architecture that lives with it. [...] I try not to do things heterogeneous to the context, but I want to build things that have a relationship of kindness with what is already there and what will be there in the future.

In your project Arumjigi, it is fascinating how you are combining traditional, contemporary, materiality, and contextual architecture...

[...] The client required to have a traditional *Hanok* inside the main building; this was his vision since the beginning... but the area was very tiny, and with strict limitations. To accommodate the traditional structure, we had to put the *Hanok* at the top level instead of its usual position - rooted on the ground. So we needed a free and pure open space to support the traditional building. I designed a very "solid" part at the upper level, playing with natural stone to recreate the "ground" and used wood materials for the *Hanok* to revive a situation similar to tradition.

Layer over layer makes the building appear differently... what is the logic behind it?

Generally speaking, I think this concept could be due to the Korean context made up of hills and mountains... This project is a sort of investigation about the organization of architectural components and how they meet each other. Also, in our tradition, the three elements - base, body, and roof - create a system that often repeats itself.

What was your strategy with respect to the context?

I did not follow it. And I was indifferent to it... but maybe not completely. It is hard to explain... For instance, if the context is very chaotic, I try to make an architecture that calms you down, but if the context is too calm, I try to make it more alive. In other words, my architecture is a reaction to the context. [...]

How did you connect the project to the public realm?

[...] In traditional architecture you access through a gate into an outer space called *"Madang"*. In the same way, you can enter the building through a courtyard surrounded by small buildings, organized by a system sustained by a sequence of relationships made of scales and composition of different elements. Here, from the public road, you can enter directly through the *"Madang"*, and after you can continue towards the exit. As a result, we have a sequence of similar voids as public spaces inside the building. [...] In the last Venice Biennale 2016 [FAR Game], the issue of building restrictions was well explained. But I tell you, if restrictions are properly used, you can create public space inside... but according to the law the inner spaces are always considered as a built area.

Crisis, Creativity, and Heritage

If you could improve the regulation, what would you do?

[...] I would change the voids definition and implement new policies to allow the construction of much more private courtyards and open spaces. As for the heights, now they are a bit deregularized, and there are more chances than before.

With so many restrictions, can architecture become more creative?

Usually, with too much freedom, you feel a sense of bewilderment. But when you are restrained, and your design is well guided, maybe... but I do not think that with restrictions you can automatically make impressive architecture, that's a different thing. [...]

How did your architecture change after 2008?

Before 2008, clients only saw constructions in monetary terms, choosing technicians rather than architects to design them. This has changed; now people are looking forward to living more comfortably, and developers are encouraged to seek for a certain cultural quality of the buildings.

What do you think is the main reason for this evolvement?

I admit the clients have evolved, but it is not due to the crisis... For instance, there is a lot of history in Italy, but in Korea, the culture was not as continuous; there were several breaking points, leaving considerable gaps in our culture. And the trace of modernity is one of them. We had built without visible references and therefore, without models, I believe we ended up without quality. Nowadays, society is different, with different tangible references. In front of Korean architects, there are the proves of better quality of life and they want to live up to that in architecture. [...] Thirty years ago, there was no chance to study architecture abroad. But after that, students have managed to do so. It was precisely in the early '90s when something started to take a turn. For example, I am one of the first generation who studied abroad, and I was the first Korean student to graduate from A.A. in London. From the 2000s, there has been a consistent and visible change due to studying and working experience abroad.

How did architecture change from the early '90s up to now?

We started little by little. Young architects began to build small buildings, a type of architecture different from commercial megaprojects of the past. We have seen the development of several competitions and their construction triggers the cultural momentum. It worked somehow, creating a new and fresh perspective... It was a blessing, and I am in favor of all the changes started from there. [...] I also very much accept foreign architects building here in Korea. It is a good drive for us... but one building is more than enough! I mean the DDP [Dongdaeum Design Plaza]. This building represents too much of the Zaha Hadid international style. Why she didn't use a higher sensitivity to the situation in Korea? But for sure, she was not going to do it; that is a pity... But from another point of view, having a building signed by Zaha Hadid... Why not?

With your various collaborations with foreign architects [Alvaro Siza and Carlos Castanheira], you have matured a good overlooking eye in understanding the possible consequences and design issues... If you had the opportunity to go back in time and advise Zaha Hadid for DDP project, what would you say?

Arumjigi
Courtesy of M.A.R.U. network

Usually, when I collaborate, my place is to only help the foreign architect... if not I would have done it myself! [Laughs]. Because my position is always to respect the thoughts of other people... I think it is the right thing to do. I can certainly give some advice, and some interpretation about some specific situations, but it depends mainly on whether they want to listen to and deal with it.

What are the main issues you are referring to?

Foreign architects coming to Korea can only understand what they see. So the results of their interpretation would be just in regards to the contemporary city. But an approach that feeds contradictory and chaotic systems will create enormous gaps in heritage and culture... If I have to give some advice, it will be to think about our history and specifics - both geographical and cultural aspects... It is not easy to understand. And even more, to consider the difference between the West and the East. Just imagine the diversity with our own neighbors like China and Japan; the Korean situation is very specific. If you are born in Korea there is always something that makes you different. For example, architects who I have worked with, Siza, Florian, and others, often made me see how modern and international I am, but somehow they describe me still as a Korean... Returning to the architectural side of the issue, to understand the situation here, one should make a great effort. It is not just about what we can or cannot see in the context, but what we can understand and also what we can get out of it. In fact, to make a more thoughtful architecture, no matter how it looks, it is what contains inside that makes the difference.

Context and Project

How does the eclectic and contradictory context generally located around your projects affect your design?

Yes, it is contradictory, but I think it is just a phase of a longer process. And in the future, it will develop into a fully grown Korean context - I hope. But at the moment it is somehow confusing. We are assisting towards a turning point of the process, and people are trying to both put it in place and direct it in a way that they want their context to be... I hope this will be visible to everyone soon. Many people were and are conditioned by a fashionable way of living, but at this moment, the situation is gradually changing and what they are now looking for is different. They are heading towards an introspective analysis of one's own personality. [...] At the moment, what we are doing is understanding what we are missing and act accordingly. Seoul, as mentioned before, is definitely a heterogeneous city, mixing tradition with contemporary but lacking in modernism... Starting from the fact that architecture is an inconsistent reinterpretation and evolution, I think it would be very difficult to translate traditional qualities into contemporary architecture. [...] In the '80s I was the coordinator of the development of Paju Book City, a milestone for the new Seoul, working together with Kim Young-Joon, Seung H-Sang, and Florian Beigan...

How did such a big project come together and how did you assume the responsibilities?

It was made by an urbanist, not an architect. Then it was subdivided... anyway, it was a very successful project, and now it is getting better with certain restrictions and guidelines.

Arumjigi
Courtesy of M.A.R.U. network

Yeosu
Courtesy of M.A.R.U. network

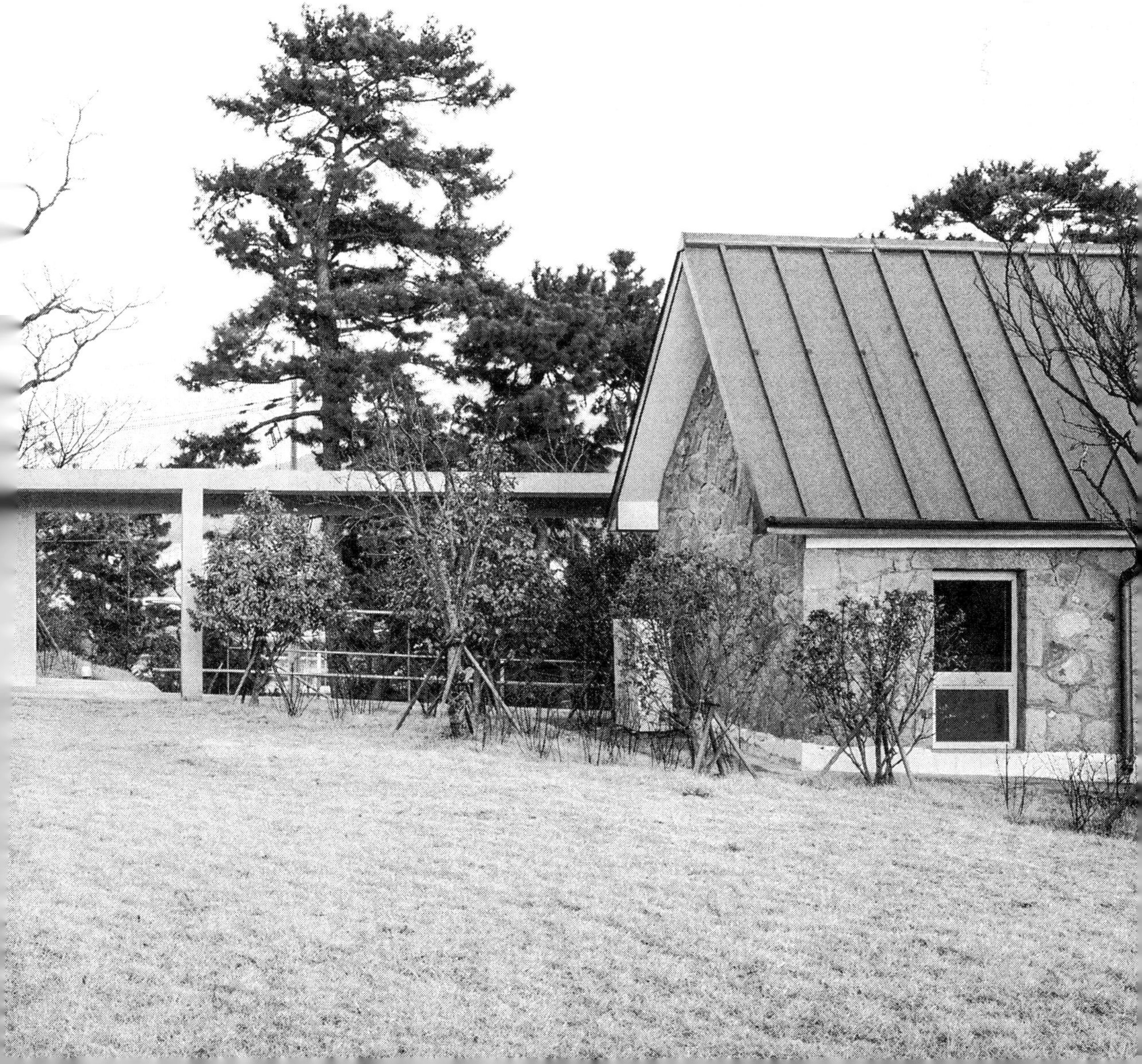

What were the main issues for you working at this project?

[...] In Korea, development has been done without taking into account any architectural aspect, but only through a very technical urban planning approach. They made an urban plan, and only when it was finished, the architects could come in and do what they had to do in freedom. When the project started, the architects created guidelines that helped - not to create a unified style - but to control the built environment. This served not only for this project but also for other parts of the city and even small towns. It was sort of a starting point; an experiment.

When it all started, Paju was pretty much an agricultural area, and then became an infrastructure framework. How do you approach such a young and plain context to start the design?

In this particular project, it's about how one imagines the city of the future, and the process to reach this result. We have to understand what methods and which criteria need to be used, and begin to understand how these criteria can be organized on-site... Surely it is related to the program, but it is also a logical process.

What about human-centered design? What kind of reaction would you like to create in people visiting your buildings?

People are the most critical aspects when I design... architecture is not made by architects for architects. I want to give people a pleasant feeling, but not a wow feeling! I want to create an environment in which people come in to have a sensation of well-being... Inside they should experience good light and good views rather than dwell on... fashionable things. I am not very into doing new experimental objects; I am not interested in this. My buildings are based on the fundamental features of space and how they can be combined to create well-being in people... I'd rather start from a very basic structure with very basic spaces, in which well-defined and simple functions are set up. When this system is defined, I gradually improve the project through several steps to find the best solutions, that's it! I am not interested in distorting shapes or finding new competitive solutions. Because a genuine architectural space is a primary space and there is no need for anything else.

"Program as an architecture generator", what is your point of view about this?

The function is a fundamental thing that you have to apply to the project, but other aspects should be taken into account as well. We don't just necessarily focus on functions, as functions could be interpreted and translated into different concepts. In architecture, there are many rules and laws that you must respect to build comparing to function, there are some other things you have to do... Then within functions, you can always have some kind of space that can be reinterpreted in different ways.... Like that, the design will be developed through different logical thoughts. [...] Function is just a basis. Once I solve it, I have to think about what I should add or interpret differently from my initial hypotheses. Space fulfills a particular function, but the feelings are different... I think space can be changed at all times. Functions are linked only to a specific time lag - as predicted - but if we have enough space quality, even if the entire function is pulled away, it will still be functional in a logical way. For this reason, I always try to give an array of multiple features and qualities to space, to perform any function needed in the future.

So how is the space actually designed to fulfill this purpose?

Yeosu
Courtesy of M.A.R.U. network

It is important to make beautiful spaces because in this way it can attract and become more functional than the particular program the space is created for. It is the fundamental thing, no matter whether it is a factory or a museum, the important thing is that they have a space that stimulates well-being, a place of potential, and more importantly beautiful... The program merely comes after spatial quality. [...] To my students, I try to teach a strategic framework of the project. Before we do a project, we have to think about what the design strategy is. In practice, what I do is to stimulate students in their own judgment and thought. They become autonomous and understand what it needs to be done case by case and step by step. The creative process is more important than the results. The results come out from the process and not the other way around. I often tell them not to come out with a predetermined image of a form, but to follow only the process that will lead to the right solution.

What message do you want to pass on to the next generation of architects?

The main thing to focus on is the way of thinking and understanding the nature of architecture. From that point, they can develop any experimentation and whatever they like, but without those fundamentals, it is difficult to produce meaningful architecture. I think what we can see and learn from this Korean condition is diversity; there are many ways to deal with a project... but if I have to give a piece of specific and final advice is go towards elegance.

I think architecture has to get closer to people's lives. Of course, it is important to explore the materials, and the way buildings are put together. But before doing so, it is essential to understand how people want to live, improve their quality of life, and live a better life within architecture.

Ken Sungjin-min
SKM Architects

How People Want to Live
Beyond the Diagrams and Concepts
Architectural Quality for All
Architecture Influences People
Legacy of Crisis, Legacy of Creativity

Ken Sungjin-min Interview
Photo by the author

How People Want to Live

I think that architecture has to get closer to people's lives. Certainly, it is important to explore the materials and how buildings are put together. But before you do this, it's also important to understand how people want to live, to improve their quality of life and to live a better life within architecture. For this reason, when we are designing a building, we must understand human beings first. This is always a question I ask, "how to be able to do things in a better way than those we did before?" "How can we make people become empowered?" I think the architectural space has the power to influence people, to bring greatness to their minds with architecture. I always try to contribute, with my life, my work, and architecture to buildings, neighborhood, and the city.

How to create a space that can influence people?

I try to bring positivity to the area where I design, to the area around, not only in everyday life when using that building but also to the people living around and to the city.

Beyond the Diagrams and Concepts

How do you define a "great architecture"?

... It cannot be explained by graphics nor diagrams, but it has to be experienced by people, by feeling the space, proportions, and light... I think not only architects, but also ordinary people, when they walk into a "great architecture" they know that even without any explanation. There is a sense of quality that people just feel. It's almost like when you go to Ronchamp; you understand immediately, and you feel that space and the kind of emotion it gives you... As well as Salk Institute with the space between the buildings that look out over the ocean. When you stand there, something really moves inside you and makes each person think differently about that moment... Architecture is an asset to all of us. Since we have limited resources in this world, I would like all the buildings to be at this same high level so everyone can enjoy a beautiful space, architecture, and city.

What are the qualities of a "Great Architecture"?

I think it's a challenging question. There is an active subjective component, and there are several needs. You have to be a good architect and have some fundamental qualities. But beyond that, there must be something profound, to touch the people who use that building. Many of these great architects have achieved these goals - like the buildings by Carlo Scarpa. When you look at his buildings, you know that he has put so much effort and soul into it. Although it is a building of another era, this place touches you, and it reaches the grandeur of art; it is a fantastic experience for people! It cannot be explained through texts or with very complicated words. Reaching this sense of quality is something that has always fascinated me.

Being able to create these grandiose architectures differs substantially from relating to a specific concept or procedure. It seems to me that you mean more like a momentum, a mental state that allows you to achieve this higher state.

Do you know the Korean game with the black-white stones called Baduk? This game has 18×18 square checkerboards, and there are hundreds of thousands of black and white stone positioning options. When you play a lot and reach a certain level, you observed an exciting thing happening. When you play, you cannot remember all the

SKM Office
Cortesy of SKM Architects

moves of your opponent, but if you look at the chessboard, you can reconstruct the sequences of the game you have been playing for even a couple of hours. You can do that only by understanding the reaction. This needs a lot of concentration, and it needs your mind to be at that moment... Sometimes I walk with my mind in the space I'm designing, I explore it and if something does not convince me I'll tell the project manager that we have to revisit that specific aspect of the project at that particular floor. Everything is based on experience! I have to focus on the environments, space, and feelings I experience. This is sometimes like old fashion architecture that is not based on section or size... I like Luis Khan's quote, "A great building must begin with the unmeasurable, must go through measurable means when it is being designed and in the end must be unmeasurable". Architecture always begins with someone's dream. It can be a dream of your home, your office or even, like it happens nowadays, to make money. Then these dreams translate into measurable things in drawings, in sections and diagrams. Then the final product is always something that is not measurable, which means that the measurable design must represent things that are not measurable such as space and relationship with people. This needs architects who put a lot of passion, soul, and thoughts into their projects. I think it's always a big challenge to reach even some aspects of this status. I do not know how to define it clearly, but all the things worth collecting or worth restoring when you look at them, you can recognize the effort that somebody put inside. But I do not think we can do all the architecture in this way, but the more you travel the more you realize the world is really small, and there is only a handful of places you can really relate to. These are places that have inspired generations of people.

Architectural Quality for All

[...] When we design we have to ask: how we want to live in this society? For this reason, I am very interested in infrastructures like subway, sidewalks, and parking spaces. It is a space used by many people every day but is not consciously developed. I think we have to look at the city with a different eye. If we do great architecture in metro stations, libraries, markets, or even shopping malls, people will feel they have been treated in a fair and worthwhile way. To do so, it does not take much money but needs a good architect.

How do you imagine a "well treated" Seoul?

Sometimes, as architects, we do not have enough power, or sometimes we feel like we cannot contribute to current society and challenges... I think cities are always very fascinating because they are one of the most expensive and vast creations of human beings. They are not just created by one person, but by the constant evolution of society... it is like life: it always evolves and improves. Some places are dying, but other places are driving towards the new development. So I'm always fascinated by what creates this dynamism in the city and the strength behind all these changes.

How would your ideal city be?

My dream city would be with a beautiful metropolitan net, designed by a great architect, with magnificent parks where people gather. My great concern is how to contribute to both the owner of a building, the people who use it and the people who pass by. Everyone needs to benefit from architecture. We live in this capitalist society where architecture has become a financial resource, but I think it is crucial to find a way in which all can work together.

SKM Office
Cortesy of SKM Architects

Architecture Influences People

Resuming one of your initial questions, I would like to ask you: How do we want to live? How to achieve good architecture in practice?

I think quality can be achieved even in a challenging environment. With the client, I always try to extend the scope of the architecture. When I design, before I jump in the next stage of the form, the materials, and the program, I try to define the actual function of the building in itself... how do we want our children to live? How do we want future generations to live? Once I designed a building for a couple. They wanted a home, and before doing anything else, we talked about life. They were that type of quarreling people that do not agree on anything. I listened to them. They wanted separate bedrooms but a shared bathroom. Even though they had their differences, they sometimes liked the discussion. Everyone has a different lifestyle, a different way of life.... As society is structured now, most people do not have the opportunity to live in the way they want. The couple lived very well together ever since and improved far more their quality of life. They told me, "we had to build this house ten years ago when we were 50!".

How do you contribute to the neighborhood?

When I grew up, my parents were Buddhists... I'm not religious, but what they were able to pass to me was the idea that I had to be an active member of the community. Everyone can contribute in so many different ways: a comedian can make people laugh, a chef can make some good food. As an architect, it is a profound challenge. I think architects can contribute in different forms: Peter Eisenman's buildings or those by Rem Koolhaas have contributed through philosophy; other architects through beautiful forms or active public spaces. My family education influenced me so much in my profession. It's a very Asian way of doing... it's like karma, what you do comes back to you. The important thing for me is to embrace nature. At my office, I have a garden in front of the entrance and another one on the rooftop. I am delighted that we are located here in this community and it is very important to me to try to help even with the smallest things for the people around me.

Legacy of Crisis, Legacy of Creativity

[...] My father had fought in the Korean War. 80% of his friends had died, and he told me about some of the sufferings he had experienced. My grandparents had suffered too under Japanese occupation. We Koreans are placed in a truly strategic position surrounded by very strong and powerful nations, and we often fall in severe crisis situations.

How do you think this has influenced you, the society, and architects?

Through the ages, we have always sought hope. The mission has always been to survive and to exist even in a critical situation. We still see the positive aspect even in situations like the economic crisis and the possibilities of fast communication and technology. We find inspiration and opportunities in the difficulties. That is why I think in Korea, many architects, even with limited resources, do not give up doing great things. This is a great value. Korea is an incubator that produces excellence: great musicians, great film directors, and writers are excellent. This comes from our difficulties and very complex history, an embedded situation within us all. [...]

SKM Office
Cortesy of SKM Architects

SKM Office
Cortesy of SKM Architects

JUNO Academy
Photos by Song Jae-young

JUNO Academy
Photos by Song Jae-young

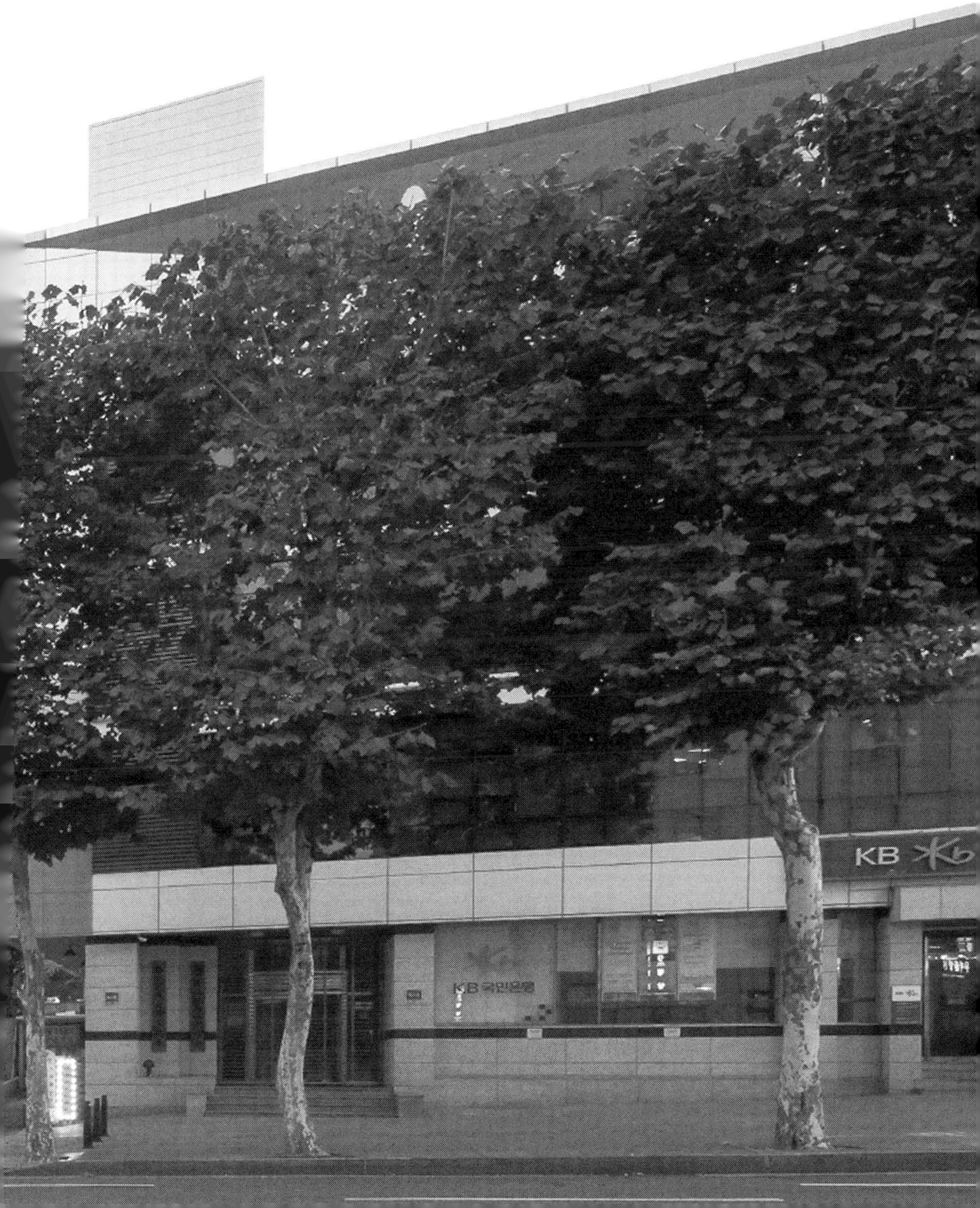

Aanti Club
Photos by Ku Boun-sook

This and next page
GS XI Gallery
Photos by Ku Boun-sook

I show clients how, with a certain procedure, they can build up a building in just two months, so they tell me: "I'll let you work!". They do not get lost in details or irrelevant comments, which can be frustrating and counterproductive... Clients always say they want to have a work of art, but this is only camouflage, it is only for communication and marketing reasons.

Kim Chan-joong,
THE_SYSTEM LAB

Materials and Modules
Quality and Practical Effectiveness
Different Type of Metabolism

Kim Chan-joong Interview
Photo by the author

Materials and Modules

[...] Our studio is very interested - or better, expert - in prefabrication... Especially in Korea, every client wants to have a quick construction to save money. In conventional construction processes, in no way you can save time! [...] How to shorten the time of construction is one of our prerogatives, so all our projects have to deal with and focus on strong prefabrication.

Your fast-paced projects - characterized by molding and prototyping techniques - are representative not only of your projects but also of all this particular situation in Korea...

[...] One of our first projects was with KKCE Construction Company. They requested a project to be designed and built in only 52 days! Usually, in our studio, we always have this type of fast-track projects, so we become real specialists in dealing with modules and methodologies like vacuum forming and other types of manufacturing. [...] This was one of our first designs, but when the rumor spread out: "these architects can build fast!" we were covered by commissions. Almost immediately, we were approached by the City of Seoul, which needed a series of pedestrian tunnel projects. 10 projects had to be designed and built within 120 days. At that time, we only had 10 people in the studio, and each person had to take care of one project. Therefore, we had decided to build the project with a polycarbonate module, to shorten up production time with a hot molding process... If we had used a conventional material, in no way could we have matched the deadline. [...] Another high-speed project had been for Samsung. This was a project of a showroom to showcase the interior of the apartments for sale. They only gave us 90 days to complete the building. This type of buildings is usually used for a short period - like six months to one year - to show information to the public and then demolished. But, even if they no longer need the building in that area, they will need it in different cities - like in Pusan and then in Jeju. So, after six months, instead of demolishing we disassembled it, transported it and rebuilt it in another location. [...] We used a polycarbonate facade again and shaped different modules to create a system easy to disassemble and very easy to transport. Looking at the shape of the modules, it might seem very random, but, in reality, if we had used a simple, flat and regular form, it would have been much more complicated. The major issue was to pull it out from the mold, which could result in a more expensive manufacturing process. Also, we didn't need to add any other structure because the shape itself increased the structural resistance which became very stable. [...] Another brand, MCM, asked us to do a renovation and creating a new interesting facade for an old building... after this 25-day project, we realized that we did not want to do any more fast design! [Laughs]. They are projects that literally kill us.

But these projects have been a boost for your career.

[Laughs]. Yes, we actually had a lot of money from them, and we have grown a lot. At the same time, if we could finish the project in even less time, the client would have given us higher fees. [...]

Tell me more about one of your slightly more conventional and lasting projects, the Flagship Store for fashion designer Paul Smith.

[...] Here, the project site was microscopic, and according to the building code, we couldn't have more space than that. This area allowed only 150%, but the

Core Hand Corporation
Photo by Kim Jae-kyeong

client wanted to have more and more! [...] So, I had an idea, I talked to Paul and told him he did not have to display everything on the ground area - increasing the necessary floor area - but he could show some shoes and clothes on the wall - only the floor area is legally counted. So we decided to blow up the upper part of the building, increasing the surface of the walls. He liked the idea, and we went ahead, creating a very full and voluminous building. [...] This building is made of reinforced concrete, but at that time, we were running out of time - as usual - so we had to figure out how to build it quickly. The main issue was the reinforced concrete walls had to follow the complex shape of the building. The surfaces were created through computerized prototyping and used blocks of 1 cubic meter of foam held together by metal plates. Even if it was a very complex structure, we could quickly produce the modules and assemble the formworks. And it was the first time worldwide - according to Architectural Review - this technique was used in architecture. [...] As you can see [showing the images of the tiny interiors] there are very small interior spaces, and he is 1.97 meters tall! [Laughs]. On the top floor, he could only walk in the middle of the room... but this space was not supposed to be here. It's extra space, for free, so that's ok...

Quality and Practical Effectiveness

Cubrick [Cube + Brick] is one of your most representative or well-known works because it represents how you treat the wall in many of your buildings...

Yes, it is an important project for me, the structure uses FRP - Fibre Reinforced Plastic. They are modules formed by the intersection between cubical and spherical shapes. [...] In reality, these elements are street furniture like benches used as an indicator of the near Modern Art Museum... The attraction mostly visited by people is the zoo - one of the largest in Korea. But they usually cannot see the museum and leave without visiting it. We were asked to design a kind of pavilion to draw attention to the museum. Always - like all my projects - the result must be very cost-effective. My strategy was, first of all, to design the benches with a very interesting shape. The cubes have been cut differently to obtain diversity and also to give different possibilities for the people to sit on. The seats were scattered along the direction of the museum, and they were regrouped, forming a bigger cube to attract more attention. One particular thing I wanted to do was to allow visiting the interior of the structure. This space, for me, is inspiring because it reminds me somehow of the spaces of a gothic cathedral - a space inside the wall that can be explored. [...] Nowadays, due to the construction technology making always thinner walls, we don't have the luxury to have this type of experience anymore...

Why are the massive walls and the spaces inside the structure so exciting for you?

The reason comes from a feeling, a personal emotion... Ok, for the Romanesque architecture the thickness of the wall is almost 1 meter, right? I really like this type of reconfiguration where the space of the wall becomes an integral part of the room. A space like this no longer exists in contemporary architecture. Yes, we can no longer use a wall thickness like the Romans did or people in the Middle Ages, but in the same way, this space with similar proportions can become attractive, maybe by putting a seat, a place for plants or maybe putting cabinets in the wall. Today we have the thickness of the wall and insulation, but the maximum depth in total is about 30cm, so it is impossible to have any

Paul Smith, Flagship Store
Photo by Kim Jae-kyeong

situation like this. [...] When I design a residential building, I often fold the edge of the window. In this way, I can have a gothic-like space, interesting, and at the same time, I can have even more space. [...] Cubrick uses the entire thickness of the wall as an architectural space. This defines new spaces inside, creating a connection with the outside.

Speaking of inside-outside connections, what are other spatial logic that creates interesting relationships in your architecture?

It depends on project by project. For example, in retail projects, I have to make unique spaces that create interesting situations. People leave the house to find something unexpected and particular, so it is something I can explore in these typologies. But if we take, for example, my residential projects, they are very conservative, so there is not a lot of freedom to do so... I like small spaces, maybe even hidden, which give a lot of privacy. I do not want to use a trendy language for the home, not even particular materials like Samsung's Pavilion or Paul Smith's showroom...

It is about effectiveness.

Right. I like exploring and using different solutions. I always question what I do, and I try to understand better the responsibility of architecture and of the architectural profession... I do not know how it works in other countries, but in Korean society, there is a fuzzy boundary between architect and artist. People usually think in this way: there are two types of architects, a more technical architect - or an architect-engineer - who does anything that the client wants, and a *"Chaka"* [architect-artist].... Considering that architecture is not done with my money, it is inevitably to be subjected to the profit. The architect does not work in the middle of nowhere, but there is always a context that we must compare to and what we design have to create a "profit" for the society. It's a fairly common thing. So I do not try to carry on a discourse that only represents my architectural language, but I persuade the client with practical reasons. I can explain that if he accepts my design, he can save both money and time, and then I can convince him of other particular ideas... I show him how, with a certain procedure, you can build up a building in just two months, so they tell me: "I'll let you work!". They do not get lost on details or insignificant comments which can be frustrating and counterproductive.... Clients always say that they want to have a piece of art, but this is just camouflage, it's just for communication and marketing reasons.

We are now in a highly repetitive residential area [Seongnam], producing a particularly alienating environment. If we compare it to districts like Jungno 3-ga, where the tight and dense environment attracts so many people, we can see how architecture profoundly affects the feeling of people, drawing activities and pushing to use spaces differently. How would do you consider this aspect when you design?

[...] I always try to produce quality in the environment through interactions. Using materiality and a distinct and unusual or beautiful form, I try to stimulate people to get closer to architecture.

I believe beauty is a very subjective and controversial topic. Do you have any personal definition?

For me, beauty is ambiguity. What interests me is not doing things that are

immediately recognizable, but architecture, on which society can project ideas based on their beliefs and thoughts... Like for the Paul Smith project, the Flagship Store. People projected ideas onto this building and said even that looks like a marshmallow or an inflatable structure! [Laughs] Since Seoul is a somewhat alienating city, and in some parts repetitive and arid of activities, I think that these elements are needed. I think we need people on the street to take a break, stop, look, and imagine.

It needs to interact with people on a different level...

Yes. Sometimes they are so interested in the building that they get closer, and start to touch it [Laughs] to understand what the surface is made of! The manager of that building told me that he really hates this! [Laughs]. I never thought that this specific thing could happen, but I think it's interesting to see how people interact differently with architecture.

From where does your concepts of "particular and ambiguous form" come from?

I think from my mother. She was a painter, and since I was a child, she often painted pictures of nudes. I observed her and tried myself. So I learned from her the composition and the aesthetic sense of beauty, especially from the human body... Also, because I always wanted to be a product designer, and to become one, you have to go through art school, but my father did not want me to. He said enough with art in the family! [Laughs] Somehow I think that my desire to become a product designer has influenced my approach to architecture, considering the shape, the efficiency, and the sensation of this building to the touch...

Different Type of Metabolism

This is Hana Bank project... You have to consider that today not a lot of people go to the bank anymore. Many things can be done online, using smartphones and online banking. This is why we had to rethink the traditional bank building. There is usually a type of traditional bank prototype that uses a lot of symmetry as huge portals and heavy languages. Our first point was to make a building that does not look like a bank. Usually, the bank closes at six, but we proposed it to be open for 24 hours to integrate many other functions into the building. The project was a renovation of a pre-existing building affected by the common speed parameters we have here in Korea. We achieve the speed by designing the structural elements of the facade in a factory and mounted on the site. The module consisted of pre-stressed concrete modules, a structure that can be self-supporting and easily assembled. It was a very complex construction process with a lot of tests, and along the way, we also thought about changing strategy, but the client was irate because he liked definitely that solution! [Laughs].

The project uses a very expressive and almost metabolic language.

Yes, it seems metabolic from the language, but it is only partially metabolic because the shape doesn't become a proper structure. Here, it is only a facade applied to an existing structure - which is missing something of the metabolic concept. I focused a lot on the facade and what it can produce both outsides and in the space between the skin and the functional space. The offices are affected by the facade. It creates outdoor areas, the curves are visible from the

Yeonhee-dong Gallery
Photo by Kim Jae-kyeong

inside, producing exciting spots. Considering it was a renovation of an ancient building we could not interact so much with the existing structure, this was an effective intervention with only a few small changes. [...]

This kind of building is somehow really linked to Korea. In Japan, I would have expected the same building to be much more minimalist... or in China much more decorative.

In some way I agree with you... you have been interviewing many Korean architects, and if I have to say it at all, I think that in the last few years the architectural language is changing. It is not anymore unified, and architects are diverging into many different directions. In the past, all the project seemed to be the same with the same values and the same results. There has always been a strict architectural rule, followed by my colleagues and academia. But now the Korean culture is changing. In Japan, they still have a strong sense of integrity with precise guidelines that come from older architects. Japan still has a strong hierarchy and young people... for example, Sou Fujimoto, is a very innovative person but I think he falls under the traditional Japanese architect category... Here, a much more complex discourse is emerging, going in many different directions. Maybe in 10 years, we will sit all together to better understand the characteristics of today's architecture. But now we are still full of experimentation... I build what I build because my clients appreciate my designs - even if they are very conservative people... some of the most respected Korean architects don't appreciate my work... without mentioning any name! [Laughs]. Especially when I run for competitions, and in commissions there is always some very respected architect, and I receive powerful criticisms. They tell me this is not architecture, it's just a game! [...]

Yeonhee-dong Gallery
Photo by Kim Jae-kyeong

I like playing with the building structure and expressing a narrative with it. I choose the facade and the interior materials in some way according to the space program, and I try to carry forward my personal aesthetic experimentation, which focuses mainly on the dematerialization of the mass through a repetition of the vertical elements.

Kim Seung-hoy
KYWC Architects

Chaos and Growth
Structure, Material and Mass

Kim Seung-hoy Interview
Photo by the author

Chaos and Growth

[...] I was born in 1963 and, at that time, the per capita income was only $100 a month. We were very poor. Now the income is $30,000 a year and still growing rapidly. Even cultural globalization has been very rapid and exponentially growing... It is a very specific situation in Seoul; all things are done at very high speeds. The clients want the buildings in a few months, from design to construction. So our architecture is always conditioned by clients, the program and the market... Especially in Korea, the urban fabric is very diverse with parts of the city built 600 years ago and other parts completed only 10 years ago. These developments have been made very quickly, with in mind the British Garden Cities and American urban planning, bringing problems related to fragmentation and alienation. Although the situation is generally chaotic, I think that the composition of our urban fabric is still a primary starting point to consider when designing... On top of the urban fabric we need to add consideration of restrictions given by clients, specifics of the program and limits of the market. In Korea, there are many types of modern, ancient, traditional and experimental buildings all mixed up together in the same spot. What we can learn from this, is that we must base our ideas and our practice on very grounded foundations, practical situations and real problems, constituting the bases of the city. [...] I didn't study only in Korea, but I also went abroad to attend the master's degree at the University of Michigan. Back then, my professors gravitated around the figure of Collin Row, and I had a fantastic experience, leaving in me a strong cultural background and historical knowledge.

How do you think your work expresses what you have learned in the United States?

The biggest influence I had was contextualism, which was widely used to support the project ideas; now, I'm inclined to use it extensively in all my projects. I really love studying classical buildings and, as you can see from this [collection of sketches from the University of Michigan], I have studied in depth the historical urban composition of both America and Europe.

In some ways these analyzes seem a vivid reminiscence of the Fascist architectural language of the 1930s...

Yes, and I also did a lot of studies on the Art Deco buildings. Thanks to these I think I had a great opportunity to have a very broad cultural background on Western architecture, also learning architectural thoughts very differently from Korean students... In all my university projects, I have always started from conceptualization of the building through an architectural idea. This was then translated into complex drawings that simultaneously represented plans, sections, elevations and views. I really loved this process, and it allowed me to have a grounded logical organization of architecture, escaping from aesthetics and forms to enter into what are the essential characteristics of space and architectural compositions.

Was the University of Michigan conservative?

I would say no. This was only part of the studies based on classical architecture, but at the same time, the university was very experimental. At the time, one of my youngest professors was 25-years-old Young Ho Chang -who later became the dean of MIT - and was the first to establish his own studio in China.

Structure, Material, and Mass

[...] When my colleagues and friends look at my buildings, they immediately understand that they were made by me. I'm honored to be recognizable, but on the other hand, I would like to escape from certain matters of style and a priori solutions... I've noticed that when I design, I'm mainly focused on some specific topics. I like playing with the building structure and expressing a narrative with it. I choose the facade and the interior materials in some way according to the space program, and I try to carry forward my personal experimentation of aesthetics, which is mainly focused on the dematerialization of the mass through a repetition of the vertical elements... [...]

[...] In a Korean situation, the architectural form is practically fixed by regulation.

Yes, mass is defined and what I do is to adapt to it. The price of the land is also very high, and the clients always want to make the maximum possible volume with what they have. There's not much we can do! I mainly deal with the skin of the building and I play with the structure... [...] For me, the structure is very important not only because it is essential for both Western and Eastern architecture, but also because it is extremely crucial for traditional architecture in Korea. In fact, in the traditional field, the wooden structural system is decisive both for the architectural composition and for the language. My intuition is to experiment with different methods on how space can be integrated into a structure, dealing with programs and the specific urban conditions we have here.

We are now in your office in the heart of Yongsan-Gu. A surprisingly expressive building even if its dimensions are very small. [...]

I think the structure is essential to give expression to the building,... I love Greek and classical Roman buildings. Structures with orders and repetitions provide a feeling of great dignity [...]. Traditional Korean buildings have a very prominent and essential wooden structure, creating interesting shapes and relationships between walls and the roof... I believe it's not just about the aesthetics of the structure, but the embodiment of their presence and strength. This is an area [Yongsan-Gu] of small compact alleys but with very high density. The office site was right at the corner of an intersection, and we could build only 9m height volume. As the first choice, we decided to go for 3m for each floor - inclusive of slabs, equipment, and structure - and I had to create an external structure to give the maximum possible height inside. The structure changes on each floor. On the ground floor, there are only three columns to provide maximum visual openness to the outside. [...] The second level is a workspace, so I used an expressive diagonal structure that recalls contemporary offices. The third level is my private office, and I designed it for a more intimate feeling. Here there are openings, framing views on specific and interesting places like the Seoul Tower, a beautiful hill or an interesting tall building. [...] I studied Mies van der Rhoe very deeply. It is interesting to observe how, starting from very modern concepts, he used well-rooted characters of traditional oriental architecture. The Seagram Building is teaching us that the structure may not only be of functional in support but may also be an essentially modern expression. In my buildings, I want to express the same thing. I never forget to be Korean because I work and live here, and I design and build my buildings here. The architecture I do is only for Seoul, and I always connect it to this city and its legacy.

In many of your buildings, you use a different language from one level to another. I could interpret this choice as an intention to create a feeling

Munhakdongne Publishers
Courtesy of KYWC Architects

or somehow propose a critique of the context made by large and massive volumes: an environment with not so many variations...

Yes, it is somehow between a critic and a realization. [...] Japan influenced us profoundly... and the Americans also. With so many external inputs - materials, languages, and architecture of different styles and eras - I intuitively always look for a particular fragmentary approach... and this fragmentation sometimes follows or interprets different uses of parts of the building.

Could we say in your case: "the material follows the function"?

Yes, in a sense, the materials express the function inside. I use warm material for private uses such as wood and terracotta and cold and high-tech ones for representative areas, etc. But there is also another aspect... If you look at Gangnam, the scale of the buildings is huge. In this area, I use different structures and different materials, dividing the building, and creating a sort of composition and scale, communicating a much more human-centered environment... At the moment I am experimenting with a particular way of doing architecture: I use materials like stainless steel to create lines on the facade.

What's the ideology behind this experimentation?

For example, in Palace J, I consider its mass not only as a solid but as a volume that can be produced by lines. [...] Lines are very different from the mass. The lines are lighter, more open... so I wanted to explore new ways of representing them. I believe the reason for this obsession is a personal intuition rather than a conclusion of some sorts. I just wonder: "how can the masses be created?" I think about playing with patterns and line repetitions, and somehow creating a vibrant architecture... I love repetitions. My favorite building in Korea is also the longest traditional building all over Asia [Jongmyo Shrine]. I believe that repetition really creates a powerful dignity, typical of classical buildings.

What did you learn from exploring these solutions?

I assume this experimentation is connected to rediscovering something lost, as a rhythm of architecture. I want a result more delicate rather than strong, because here we have many buildings that literally "scream" [eclectic architecture of Gangnam]!. I desire to go against this trend, creating an empty feeling rather than a full one... The lines create small spaces, let the light play differently on the surface... In architecture, I enjoy having fun and explore... I don't know if you can learn from, or if there is anything essentially Korean - or universal - in my architecture.

Munhakdongne Publishers
Courtesy of KYWC Architects

This and next page
Soyul
Courtesy of KYWC Architects

What we can do is just "survival architecture". We can only point towards an architecture that makes sense in a rapidly changing environment, with low budgets, and high technical standards... I make architecture for me, for my clients and I do the best I can.

Lee Jeong-hoon
JOHO Architecture

Identity Controversy, Budget, and Crisis
A Matter of Culture
Understanding Your Own Culture
The Opportunity is Now
City, Seoul, and Context

Lee Jeong-hoon Interview
Photo by the author

Identity Controversy, Budget, and Crisis

[...] Korea is changing rapidly; we design quickly and demolish even faster. Now we are in the era of a high-level lifestyle when people are always looking for a new trend... If on the one hand, this progress is a positive point, on the other hand, this has also caused a severe crisis in the field of architecture. [...] I'm now in my 40s - in my fifteenth year in the field - and like most senior architects, I had numerous problems to overcome, such as the wave of "rapid changes in architecture"... This requires you to think, create, and adapt quickly to client's needs. [...] I believe that constant change is a challenging but positive aspect, and for resourceful and creative people there are many opportunities here. [...]

How has the market changed since the economic crisis?

I have more projects now... Some time ago, the trend was always to look for something new. With economic growth, Korean clients were always looking at global architects like Zaha Hadid, OMA, and Jean Nouvelle. Politicians have used architecture to ingratiate themselves with people and get more votes. Similarly, in the private sector, wealthy and powerful companies like Samsung and Hyundai are always trying to find innovative and internationally renowned architects. However, now, it's changing again. Nowadays, clients are looking for capable local people, but able to achieve international quality. Therefore, we have much more projects now...

Why do you think the developers made this move? It seems that, at the same time, they have gone from the simple iconic or luxury to an innovative design approach...

During my grandfather's era, the clients were not culturally "aware". They were influenced by fashion, and they were pretty naive. With their decisions, they caused a problematic cultural delay, putting Korea behind the global stage, leading the nation rapidly into crisis. However, subsequent events have changed their minds. They soon realized they needed foreign architects, using sophisticated technologies and expensive solutions to raise the level of architecture... In my experience, the relationship between the client and foreign architects is different; famous international architects are used to receiving great respect from their clients. In Korea, however, cultural etiquette requires architects to be more subject to client's requests, placing them at a much lower hierarchical level. It is tied to tradition... For example, here, clients may want foreign architects to visit Korea even for a simple meeting and, if they refused, clients could get very angry... Instead, Korean architects could never refuse availability because of the respect of the rigid hierarchy of society. Consequentially, clients gravitated much more towards local architects. [...] If we go back in time, Korea has never had a specific term to express "architect". There were only people called carpenters. [...] Clients have now changed their perspective, and are more inclined to work with architects like me who have studied abroad and can do the same international architecture - but being available and observant of the hierarchy. [...] My grandfather's or my father's generation never went abroad. It was up to the government to authorize the trip, and the possibilities were rare... In 1988 there were the Olympic Games in Korea, and from there, the government softened the restrictions, giving more freedom to travel. People who went abroad came back with opened eyes, ready to embrace the contemporary trends to the fullest. The wealthy class began to understand and appreciate good architecture, and this was a critical factor in the recent national development. Important people bet on young and brilliant minds with international experience and education - people of my age are already CEOs of very powerful companies. [...]

Nine Bridge Pergola
Courtesy of Joho Architecture

A Matter of Culture

[...] In my opinion, most of the architects who built after the Second World War were very busy building very quickly, and they never thought of understanding what modernization really was and what it really represented. They used only quick and ready solutions from the United States, leading to just "buildings", but not "architecture". At that precise moment, we lost our way.

Is there any "responsibility" for the Korean architects to bear now?

In the case of Japanese architecture, there is a deep connection between the architects of each generation. But here it is missing... In particular, I've noticed how in the Japanese architecture, the interpretation of the tradition becomes the dominant design motif, coming together to create a sort of Japanese architectural style. But in Korean architecture, this link between generations is somehow missing... I think this is the obstacle we have to overcome. [...] Our generation is making an attempt to translate the qualities of traditional architecture into a style or a new movement... When I was working in Paris for Shigeru Ban, in the office, I saw a book called Atlas Architecture, showcasing the architecture from all around the world. The Japanese and Chinese architecture section were very large, but the Korean part consisted of just a few pages. [...] So I tried to think, somehow as if I were a western editor and wondered, "what is the difference between Japanese and Korean architecture?"... I think Japan has a strong identity. It comes from tradition and has managed to relate to international modernity. [...] For example, Ando Tadao, although he was strongly influenced by Le Corbusier, created his own interpretation of Japanese style. I think this attitude is very critical and essential for the debate. [...] Their architectural style is not only Japanese, but it is genuinely international and at the same time different from the Western style. I think we don't have the strength to create a movement like Japan had created... or maybe that moment is far gone!

Why can't architects create a strong impact here?

We must accept reality: we have lost the way to modernize architecture. We are still creating something but, from an international point of view, it is not so relevant. Sometimes I ask myself, "why has Japan been so successful, and why should we be different?". Thus, the role of my generation could also be to find an answer to this question.

How do you think the cultural heritage is changing?

Yes, it's changing, but It's just a matter of culture, and you can see it reflected in the built environment. Now the clients are raising the bar. They look up on the internet and see architecture from other countries. They visit famous buildings abroad and send reference images back. In all these dynamics, you know, we cannot have the "luxury" to discuss identity issues. What I can do is to understand how to be an international architect first to have a chance to fulfill the requests of my clients. [...] I'm pragmatic; I'm committed to go to all the events of architecture around the world - to the Venice Biennale, Design weeks, etc. - to always try to stay familiar with every new international trend and maintain good relations with international colleagues... My aspiration is not to be globalized but to survive this harsh Korean condition.[...]

Let's take a few steps back away from this stimulating but complicated subject,

Nine Bridge Pergola
Courtesy of Joho Architecture

and talk about how you personally approach design. How do you achieve meaningful architecture?

Our understanding of "meaningful architecture" differs widely from what the clients have in mind. In this condition, what we can do is only "survival architecture". We can only point towards an architecture that makes sense in a fast-changing environment, with low budgets, and high technical standards... I make architecture for me, for my clients, and I do the best I can...

Understanding Your Own Culture

I always wanted to study at a European university. I was fascinated by the European history and by the great tradition of theory and philosophy... In 1998 I got the scholarship to go to France, and I left Korea. I really enjoyed living and studying in France. At university, I was a passionate student, reading theoretical essays by Peter Eisenman, Christian Norberg Schulz, and many others. All these experiences have pushed me in a certain direction... I know it's somewhat contradictory that when you try to define your identity you need to look abroad and then realizing it. I changed my mind; I was westernized! [Laughs]... Now I have several friends, both Italian and French. I like Espresso, French Croissant, I like cheese and wine. I feel half Asian and half European. In the same way, I deal with architecture; I always wonder what a person with different backgrounds might think, and I explore new design solutions.

What could be current aspect in Korean architectural identity?

Do you know K-Pop? This music is becoming a very interesting phenomenon in the international pop culture scene, but it could be useful as well to make a point about architecture... When I was a child, I admired Hong Kong actors, and Jackie Chen was my idol! Koreans have had significant influence from Hong Kong, from music and movies; we even dressed like them! But 20 years ago everything has changed, our culture has somehow reached a certain level. We have opened our market in Hong Kong and Japan, and now, our neighbors are the ones looking back to us, listening to K-Pop music and watching the Korean soap operas...

The Opportunity is Now

90% of the architects I know that have graduated from Harvard or Columbia, they find themselves in a tough situation. They came back to Korea to open their offices, finding opportunities but a highly competitive market. [...] In my studio, I do things very pragmatically. I have to come up always with something new for my clients. I have to define my own identity - or unique feature - to distinguish myself from the mass.

Your situation is quite fortunate. It's tough, yes, but it allows your generation to create something decidedly new...

It's true. This is the time to find the "new way". Clients want new things, and this allows experimentations. I think the problem with my colleagues is they cannot face limitations, but they want to accomplish projects of high impact right away. The big problem is the budget. Clients do not have that kind of money available for something extreme. So, how can we find a way to create a new building's identity with such limitations?... You have to be smart!

Namhae Chema House
Courtesy of Joho Architecture

How to be smart in a pragmatic approach?

The main thing is to understand where to put your energies. We must choose what to focus on and make compromises. It can be a particular detail of the facade, the use of a specific material... but you can't do everything! Let me show you a project [Namhae House Renovation]. I built it as soon I opened my studio 8 years ago. It was a renovation of a small house in the countryside, a project with a very low budget. The primary material was a metal fence applied to the facade. We chose it because the supplier told us he could not sell it, so we use it for the design, and it came out very cheap! [Laughs] [...] The project was straightforward but had its complexity. We kept the old structure, and we modeled a curved facade using only the wire mesh. In just a week, we finished the project. A strong image with a very low budget - like the client wanted.

A pragmatic way of building...

Yes exactly, being pragmatic to create extraordinary things. Nobody wanted to build it except me! [Laughs]

City, Seoul, and Context

What are the essential characteristics of an ideal Korean city?

It's a challenging question... Our context has been influenced by American cities like Chicago, based on repetitive, rectangular plots... The streets of nam are the results - an environment not made for people. [...] Seoul is too dense, and the human scale is missing. Many districts are hyper-developed without enough public space. We need open spaces... not just parks - usually underused and not very accessible to people - but spaces with public functions and activities well integrated into the urban tissue. As an architect, I'm pushing in this direction... Let's take the car and go not far from here. I want to show you the exhibition space and shops I just built for Louis Quatorze [Platform L] which deals with these kinds of spaces...

[Arrived at the Platform L] It has an unusual and distinct image, and it stands out from the surroundings... What is the concept behind it?

You see how it invites people to come in? I integrated a courtyard in the center, a multifunctional space as a sort of piazza where different activities come together [...]. The main client is a manufacturer of women's bags. The company logo is the symbol of the 14th king of France, and the concept plays around this theme. King Louis Quatorze was the one who promoted the French baroque and classified the standards of beauty, encouraging art and architecture. He defined calligraphy through geometry and proportions - elements also visible in the palace of Versailles... I found inspiration from geometric symbols: in the interior, I tried to use simple absolute geometries, while for the facade, I used complex geometries... These elements are not literal but interpreted throughout a Korean way... [...] On the facade the pattern of circulation overlaps within the facade, using quite simple and cheap materials but producing an impressive textile-like complexity. [...] We are Gangnam; It is an exceptional situation! In the '80s the City of Seoul developed this area in an extremely orthogonal grid - based on the logic of vehicular transport. It is in total contrast to the northern and ancient part of the city, where the small alleys and intricate layout can comfortably accommodate activities - more museums and exhibitional spaces. It's the first museum of its kind in Gangnam, and I wanted to create a space as a culture generator. [...] The

Namhae Chema House
Courtesy of Joho Architecture

design revolves around empty spaces, trying to create a relatively large public space inside. In the underground, there are several compartments, but when the walls are removed, we can have a completely empty space... It can be used for many activities, for exhibitions, fashion shows, etc. You see, I created an outdoor courtyard and an internal public space where public functions are ensured... It's not just empty, it's very versatile.

[Climbing up the building] From this terrace, we can see a truly schizophrenic context all around...

Yes, in Gangnam there is a taste for very eclectic styles! [Laughs] Clients want to build expressive buildings, hoping to earn more from sales and leases. I'm strongly against mere symbols and forms... If you look around, there are so many exaggerated facades that you can't really understand what's going on! Right now it's a very eclectic historical period... but we have to build a new architectural discourse for the future.

So, what to do now?

I'm not for demolishing, but I'm for minimal interventions here and there... I would try to keep as much as possible. Because, if we destroy the physical traces – no matter good or bad they are - there will never be a relationship between the past and future. When you see Milan, Paris or London, we can read the city and recognize the different ages. This is why there are so many tourists who want to visit these cities - and this clearly shows their spatial quality. We must consider all aspects and our specific problematic situations. In this way, we can preserve and emphasize our historical layers. [...] We must be "transgressive" and build a different context. We have to show the narrative of architecture! I think the narration is the main element of a thriving city, bringing out the history of architecture and transform it into the future.

Plaform L
Contemporary Art Center
Courtesy of Joho Architecture

The Curving House
Courtesy of Joho Architecture

The Curving House
Courtesy of Joho Architecture

The Issues of Seoul Architecture

by Pier AlessioRizzardi

Rem Koolhaas vs Kenneth Frampton
The "Discourse-Machine"

Bearing Wall vs Post and Beam
A Solution to FAR Game

Public Realm vs Courtyard
Void, Porosity and Public Space

Structural Expressionism vs Alienation
A Solution for Identity

Form vs Shape
The Path to Simplicity

Fascination vs Reference
Hanok for Contemporary Architecture

Nostalgia vs Legacy Revival
Renovation, Reconstruction, Replication

Artificial vs Natural
The Maximum Impact of the Minimum Intervention

Contextualism vs Tabula Rasa
Starting from What is Missing

Rem Koolhaas vs Kenneth Frampton
The "Discourse-Machine"

The Koreanness is used both to infuse identity in buildings and as a brand to give immediate value to the project by designers with little time available or lower cultural knowledge.

To achieve this goal, architects work with spatial composition and materiality. The architectural composition focuses on spatial relationships that produce private spaces balanced with areas of socialization, while materiality is expressed by the "rough" approach, represented by the 4.3 Group. Low-tech construction methods, using natural materials, and a design approach focused on letting atmospheric elements cause erosion and oxidation, bring beauty out of architecture.

When the user interacts with architecture, architects work with the interpretation of a ceremony of gestures coming from traditional culture. They try to design spaces that can change the user's sensations to alter the dynamics and internal speed - the changed behaviours could put the users into different relationships with architecture and positively influence the activities inside.

In practice, Koreanness is more a support for planning than a strict guideline. The supporters of the identity try to pursue and understand the cultural, social, and historical values to offer to the contemporary architectural framework. In the last decade, we can observe a shift and attempt to depart from these delicate issues, which are a controversial field of actions and somehow retrograde by the most progressive international community – which, at the same time, remains an excellent tool for success and publicity.

It is a logic that does not differ much from what is already established both in Asia and internationally. In current practices, we can observe the duality between the escape from the dynamics of the "discourse-machine" and the various "-ness", putting young architects at the risk of falling into the trap of mediocrity, and the possible fame and chances of winning competitions and prizes that the search for identity can provide.

It is clear to see how the "discourse-machine" is currently flooding all exhibitions and architectural publications, forming a globalized situation, a levelling of the culture, producing similar outcomes worldwide. Most of the buildings on display insist on materiality, low-tech approaches, and contextual design that generate the opposite results of the architect's original intent.

The same problem can be seen in the field of cinema in which the directors who use tradition and historical plots are rewarded in most international film festivals, and the same happens in the artistic field with young artists, describing the destruction of the legacy or covering traditional themes, to quickly gain international fame.

Recently, something is awakening in the film industry. Park Chan Wook created the internationally acclaimed contemporary movie titled "Old Boy", opening the discussion on another type of identity that differs from the tradition, clashing with the contemporary urban environment. Likewise, some of the interviewed architects tackle with issues that go far beyond traditional wooden houses, addressing the k-Pop culture and the "schizophrenic" urban context, based on consumerism and mass production.

The two factions are composed of critic and post-critic architects, both with an intention of creating meaningful architecture, but some based on the rediscovery of traces of tradition and heroically trying to change the society, while some others accept the current situation as it is and try to make the best of it. This represents a complex and contradictory discourse that has filled already thousands of pages and has not yet found an answer either at Korean, Asian, or world level.

Bearing Wall vs Post and Beam
A Solution to FAR Game

'Porous Facades'
As previously credited

The skin of the building becomes an element to be explored through concepts of physical and visual connections, drawing on the notions of traditional architecture. The architects observe and criticize the contemporary architecture intended as an influence coming from the West. They compare the western bearing wall structure to the columns and beams of the eastern one and to differentiate the local architecture, they insist on the proportion of the walls and facades.

In contemporary architecture, the walls measure about 30 cm, including insulation, pipes, and structures, and there are not many possible spatial innovations in this small space. Influenced by the rules of the FAR game, working in the "grey area" of the Korean code, architects try to challenge the proportions of the wall by revisiting the separation and layering of the elements of the wall. Expanding the space of the wall and separating the structure from the facade, they try to create a new interface between inside and outside, leaving room for new relationships, dynamics, and new possible functions.

The result is a new interface, a marginal space in which the facade receives a new potential. The architects undertake the task to explore this new potential, thus referring to a traditional interior and exterior connection, the need for novelty and innovation, and to support the changing dynamics of relationships of the program.

Public Realm vs Courtyard
Void, Porosity and Public Space

'The Power of Void'
As previously credited

The empty space represents a characteristic that remains unchanged across Korean, Chinese, and Japanese culture, describing one of the most profoundly, culturally and historically rooted aspects in Asia.

The contemporary city is extraordinarily dense and lacks empty areas and public spaces. The architects remember the 60s and 70s when cars were very rare, and the streets became spaces for public aggregation. With the rapid growth of the 80s, the government was not sensitive and unable to maintain relations between the city and the empty spaces. Effective policies were missing, incapable of stimulating new public spaces in step with the new historical period.

Now architects have detected the missing public space as one of the most important features and seek to find new solutions for its scarcity. They try to look back at the basics of the traditional structure of the *Hanok,* translating the dynamics of the private courtyard to the rules of the public realm, revealing the "edge" between nature and artefacts as a new topic of discussion to solve the problem. Working with opposite elements of emptiness and fullness, man and nature, the artificial and the natural, they interpret in between stylistic elements of Eastern philosophy derived from Taoism expressed by Yin and Yang.

From an extended point of view, the consideration of the void, in its various forms and interpretations, is something also rooted in the international culture - observing the experimental cases of the Mat buildings, Team X, Aldo van Eyck, and Megastructures of the 70s. This brings the concept of the void to be both widely revered and accepted in Asia and by international theorists and critics, boosting its application to the local Korean context. The downside is a superficial use of the void, becoming just "label" to attach to the project, fuelling the design with laziness, irrelevant results, and low-quality public spaces. Instead, we see how the void - thus public space - assumes quality when this becomes an integral part of architecture mass and serves as a link between itself and outside to the urban space.

The examples of Ssamziegil building, in Insadong district, created a potential to generate a public attraction so strong as to be almost unmanageable by its owners, promoting new pedestrian dynamics and influencing neighbouring buildings and activities around. In this situation, it can be observed how the building is declassified, and the attention shifts to the void that is not conventionally considered architecture.

The void in between architecture becomes the most important, unpredictable, potentially more active to create new dynamics and programs, revealing itself as an all-encompassing main compositional principle of architecture, expanding the architectural research from the single building to an urban system and the city based on a housing system.

Structural Expressionism vs Alienation
A Solution for Identity

'Structural Expressionism'
As previously credited

Going towards regionalism and achieving the quality using simplicity, and nostalgic terms, architects find themselves facing problems of a sterile, minimal, and over-simplified environment that run the risk of creating alienating spaces. To solve the problem, they use a mannerism of architectural elements, tectonics, and structural expressionism with a traditional taste. The Regional-Critical architects observe the past and transcribe the distinctive features of traditional architecture: the modularity of the wooden structure, the sculptural structure of the roof, and the lack of a facade - unlike Western architecture. They recognize that the structure represents the major archetype of traditional architecture,

represented by a fusion of decoration, structure, and repetition. In their works, the structural archetype evolves, and takes into account contemporary problems and needs to create a forward-looking architecture.

The theory behind the architects' approach draws on both the history of local and international architecture, starting from local example to end up in an extensive list of sources, including the classic Ludwig Mies van der Rohe's structural languages, and Frank Lloyd Wright's use of organic modularity. With a broadened point of view coming from inside and outside their culture, they criticize both the Western and the Eastern models, to find their interpretative vision, of what architecture needs today.

Form vs Shape
The Path to Simplicity

'Minimalism and Details'
As previously credited

The mega-developments programs of the 80s, corruption, illegal construction and dictatorship were the driving factors behind the repetitiveness and alienation of the contemporary residential construction panorama.

The architects grew up surrounded by non-places. They've noticed that spatial simplicity of the 80s is no longer able to support people's current needs and complexities of contemporary life. To characterize a space without any historical stratification, they use complex strategies, through evolutionary processes and aggregative composition, in combination with the marginal space of the facade.

This experiment takes place through the exploration of new types of tectonics through the continuity of architectural elements and physical connections. The skin becomes an improved interface between exterior and interior, taking on a new role as an incubator of new spatial compositions and social relationships. The facade becomes a controversial topic of discussion, providing both new inputs to enhance the design practice and critics about the temptation of creating meaningless projects based on the shape of the building.

Seoul has the problem of having areas touched by chaotic and inconsistent developments, especially in areas where corruption and illegal construction have been perpetuated for a long time. Due to the regularity of the residential bubbles, the architects face the chaotic situation, engaging in the simplicity of the design solutions and in the tendencies to regularize the masses of the buildings, proposing new coherent urban fabrics.

In both simple and complex approaches, the form tends to be viewed negatively and interpreted as a means for its own sake, embodying a symbol of construction of speculation, ignorance, and indifference to the urban environment. In line with international criticism, the standardized approach pushes architects to shift the focus from form to space, converging on a compositional complexity and heterogeneous spatial dynamics rather than recognizable and iconic forms.

Among the intellectual orthodox architects, the facade receives less importance and becomes a secondary aspect. Architecture loses the decorative and extravagant features of the previous decades to find a balance with the context, creating forms that do not impose themselves on the architectural landscape. Whether for simplicity or complexity, the architects support the issue theoretically, reconnecting to tradition through minimalism of textures and "without a facade" architecture in which the building is designed only through spatial qualities of physical and visual connection.

With an architecture based on the reactions of the users and the narrative of the spaces, they pay much more attention to the sensory aspect of the architectural space, including comfort and discomfort, designed fragility and solidity, smells and tactile sensations. These considerations lead to an architecture generated around the sequence of empty and full space and the alternation between nature and artifice.

Fascination vs Reference
Hanok for Contemporary Architecture

'Deleuzian Fold'
As previously credited

Although intellectual architects generally avoid talking about a direct influence from Hanoks, they grew up in them, and from the interviews, it transpires a fascination by multilevel structures, the sequences of spaces and the void, leaving traces along with their architectural production. Many features of Korean Hanoks echo in between Japanese *Minka* and Chinese *Siheyuan*. Going deeper into the understanding in its essential characteristics could be useful to observe the differences and similarities between them based on the culture and society metanarratives. China has always had a powerful imperial government that reflects in the large-scale and spectacular architecture, formed by sequences of large, iconic, and monumental spaces where buildings have little to do with the human scale. In Japan, everything is much smaller and more subdued, generating architectures of refined simplicity in which the human scale becomes a constraint that gives little freedom of interpretation. The Korean *Hanok* remains halfway between the two typologies, considering the scale and the levels of privacy.

The *Ondol*, the floor structured according to the technology of floor heating - represents a complex three-dimensional composition missing from both China and Japan. The *Ondol* system creates a development with increasing levels to employ the natural pattern of the vapors coming from the fireplace and reaching the sleeping area. The different levels reduce the need for furniture and enhancing the "poor" essentiality of the space. The intelligentsia explains the use of three-dimensional complexity tendency by the conformation of the vast mountainous terrain in Korea, a distinctive character of the city of Seoul. One frequently discussed example by the architects is Frank Lloyd Wright's Taliesin House, which takes influence from these typologies, importing the volumetric complexity into the United States in the 40s.

In addition to volumetric composition, architects study *Hanoks* in terms of feelings and relationships between building and the human body. They also reflect on how people can connect to space through narrative experience, recurring gestures, and domestic routine.

The *Hanok* is not properly a place for solitary contemplation like in Japan or sculpture admiration like in China, but it uses alternating situations of privacy and spatial connectivity that could be definable by Piranesian characteristics; It is a system based on the perception including and integrating the nature in the building layout. Thanks to the superimposed contrast of many geometries and spatial qualities, the archetype of the *Hanok* is affirmed as a model to be applied and revisited in contemporary architecture, which feeds the production of innovative and flexible spaces with intrinsic spatial qualities.

The model, thus applied to contemporary architecture, multiplies different experimentations, creating spontaneous and exciting design solutions - vertical movements, sliding walls and contrasting elements - influencing the vital rhythm of the users and their mood.

Nostalgia vs Legacy Revival
Renovation, Reconstruction, Replication

'Deleuzian Fold'
As previously credited

With traditional architecture challenging to preserve and with a rapid transition between medieval and modern architecture, restoration is a sensitive subject in Korea. Historically in Asia, the ephemeral is preferred over permanent artefacts, materializing Taoist philosophy at the base of traditional local culture. The result is a different approach to restoration trends from in the West. When intellectual-architects return home from experiences in Western universities, the discourse evolves, becoming contradictory, delicate and exciting clashes with the theme of the restoration of the legacy from the last 50 years and the reconstruction of traditional buildings already completely replaced piece by piece over the centuries. Here they are faced with the dilemma of how to improve their heritage without creating clichés, "Postmodern Pastiche" or giving up by considering it a lost battle.

The most prolific architects research for new theories capable of supporting new ideas of restoration, taking into consideration the current local conditions. This "nostalgic-of-action" observes the populist criticisms of disapproval, considering them senseless and retrograde. Referring to local examples such as the national treasure of the south gate of Seoul, destroyed and then completely rebuilt as it was, they described in the UNESCO directives, defining the guidelines for an authentic architecture: it is not about the authenticity of the material used by the authenticity of the design, which makes medieval temples rebuilt year after year, or even relocated, authentic in any way.

Bogus national and international critics - or failed intellectuals - criticize these methods, forgetting similar examples in their own countries. The historical reconstruction is not only relegated to Asia, but natural calamities and wars have always destroyed the European legacy and the approach of rebuilding "where it was, as it was" was perpetrated several times- such as the bell tower of San Marco in Venice rebuilt after an earthquake, keeping the same appearance of the original one and fooling everybody visiting the city. This aspect could lay the foundations for a new discussion to reflect on what can be considered original both in Asia and in the world, as the very foundation of originality at the base of architecture and heritage. Although hanging towards the favour of critical regionalism, the dilemma remains open, giving, in recent years, the possibility to intellectuals to engage in a solitary-heroic reconstruction of the past, a chance to fight the outdated status quo.

Artificial vs Natural
The Maximum Impact of the Minimum Intervention

'Natural Nature Ideal'
1-4. Photo by Aleksandr Zykov
2-3-5-7. Photo by the author
6. Photo by Eco Dalla Luna
8. Photo by Francisco Anzola

Traditionally, instead of "constructing architecture", the expression "putting a building on the ground" is used. This wording is indicative of a particular philosophical approach concerning how space can not be transformed but can be only borrowed from nature. In these terms, nature becomes an element beyond time and comprehension, to be considered as something immutable even with the human action: "we live in nature and are therefore part of it". Korean nature is substantially different from Chinese and Japanese. The traditional Chinese gardens are a manifestation of a hyper-realized nature, perfectly balanced to the standards of artistic beauty, ending up as a composition impossible to recognize in nature. Also, the Japanese minimal and idealized nature is impossible to be seen outside the human made realm. Korean nature, on the other hand, as in its traditional art and architecture, is understood as raw and unrefined. Korean gardens become intentionally indistinguishable from the natural realm, enhancing the qualities of imperfection and natural effects.

Contextualism vs Tabula Rasa
Starting from What is Missing

'Context Generetor'
As previously credited

The complexity of the context in Korea cannot be studied with only parameters derived from a western theory. Realizing that it is an almost impossible goal to describe the Korean context, architects try to discover new logics beyond what they have learned and what is being practiced. Contextual complexity is used to design alternative spatial logics and the unpredictability of interior spaces as an attempt to simulate a continuous discovery and positively influence the exploration of space by users.

On the other hand, the Critical-Architects strive to find a connection on what little remains tangible and visible. The current condition is considered the most significant, and they heroically attempt to pursue historical and cultural research and apply even small results in design solutions.

Strangely, where the context does not exist - in the Western understanding of the term - they consider the context even more relevant. Intellectual-Architects, with a solid European background, observe the current Non-Context and compare it with a personal and idealized one - which could only exist in their mind and the memories of their experiences abroad - they observe the differences and the consequent shortcomings. The experimental exercise identifies missing elements and inconsistencies

that can be solved through their projects, trying to converge towards a contextual idealization similar to the European one.

With a highly pragmatic and conscious approach, aware of the implementation of these difficulties, architects do not claim to have the power to revolutionize the situation completely, but their objectives are based on the attempt to trigger a chain reaction, hoping to influence the surrounding area positively.

It is interesting to observe the contradictory nature of this approach: starting from contextual concepts, the result grows in anti-contextual, where architects add alien and non-characteristic elements, to that particular area, drawing on self-referential elements, ideal visions, and contexts that have never existed.

Starting from what to avoid in the current condition and having a catalog in mind of good practices, a multitude of new architectural creative practices is generated. One of the generalized problems present in the European and Western peripheries is a copy of the copy of neighboring buildings, reproduced through simplifications of their characteristic elements and distant from any architectural quality. This is quickly transforming the recent urban landscape into a meaningless relationship that would never have the power to create tomorrow's context.

Burge, Russell. "Seoul: Memory, Reinvention, and the Korean Wave by Ross King." Seoul Journal of Korean Studies 31, no. 2, 2018.

Ching, Francis DK, Mark M. Jarzombek, and Vikramaditya Prakash. A global history of architecture. John Wiley & Sons, 2017.

Choi, Jae-Soon, ed. Hanoak: traditional Korean homes. Hollym International, 1999.

D. K. Forbes and S. Hamnett, Planning Asian cities: risks and resilience. Abingdon, Oxon: Routledge, 2013.

Ddp Dress in Seoul. Gyeonggi-Do. Nemo Factory, 2016.

F. Sanin. Seoul scenarios: Seoul. Space Books, 2005.

H. Pai and M. Cho, Crows eye view the Korean Peninsula; 14. International Architecture Exhibition - la Biennale di Venezia ;Seoul: Archilife, 2014.

I. Jung and C. Maniaque-Benton, Point - counterpoint Point - contrepoint: trajectories of ten Korean architects: trajectoires de dix architectes coréens. Copenhagen: Architectural Publisher B, 2014.

Iwatate, Marcia, and Kim Unsoo. Korea style. Tuttle Publishing, 2012.

J. Busquets. Deconstruction/construction: the Cheonggyecheon Restoration Project in Seoul. Cambridge, MA: Harvard University Graduate School of Design, 2011.

J. J. Seong. Seoul architecture. Seoul: CA Press, 2007.

J. Kim and S.-C. Choe, Seoul: the making of a metropolis. Chichester: J. Wiley, 1997.

J. Kim and S.-C. Choe. Seoul: the making of a metropolis. Chichester: J. Wiley, 1997.

J. Lim, S. L. Ryoo, C. A. Mouat, and B. Jackson, K-architecture: tradition meets modernity. Korea: Korean Culture and Information Service, Ministry of Culture, Sports and Tourism, 2013.

Jackson, Ben, and Robert Koehler. Korean Architecture: Breathing with Nature. Vol. 12. Seoul Selection, 2015.

Joo, N. C. "History of Korean architecture." 2000.

Jung, Inha. Architecture and urbanism in modern Korea. University of Hawai'i Press, 2013.

Kal, Hong. Aesthetic constructions of Korean nationalism: Spectacle, politics and history. Routledge, 2011.

Kim, Sung Hong. Contemporary Korean Architecture: Megacity Network. Jovis, 2008.

Kim, Sung Hong. The Far Game: Constraints Sparking Creativity: the Korean Pavilion Biennale Architettura 2016, Space Books, 2016.

P. Dechow, K. Gothe, and Yi Sook-choong. Seoul Living Lab: urban planning & design. Stuttgart: Avedition, 2017.

P. G. Rowe. Emergent architectural territories in East Asian cities. Birkhäuser, 2011.

P. W. Ferretto, Place/Seoul. Seoul: Propaganda, 2016.

Park, Jinhee, and John Hong. Convergent flux: contemporary architecture and urbanism in Korea. Walter de Gruyter, 2012.

Seoul. London: Phaidon, 2012.

Youn, Seung Ho. "The Impact of the Colonial Architectural Heritage on South Koreans' National Identity." PhD diss., University of Surrey, 2014.

Yun, Jieheerah. Globalizing Seoul: The City's Cultural and Urban Change. Routledge, 2017.

data.oecd.orgiempiself-employment-rate.htm

data.seoul.go.kr

data.worldbank.org

dev.vworld.kridev

factfinder.census.gov

kosis.kr

open.eais.go.kr

www.metro.tokyo.jp

www.nsic.go.krindsi

www.toukei.metro.tokyo.jp

www.visionofbritain.org.uk

Acknowledgments

This volume could not be created without:

- The initiative of Rafael Luna to make this project happen;
- The trust of Iwan Baan to support the publication;
- The determination of Choi Won-Joon, John Hon, Caroline Maniaque to describing the condition of Soul vividly;
- The support of l'ARCA international Magazine and Cesare Maria Casati, of STUDIO Architecture and Urbanism Magazine with Romolo Calabrese;
- The intelligence of Zhang Hankun, as essential support to research;

Printed in Great Britain
by Amazon

61992799R00322